Contemplative Gardening

Contemplative GARDENING

Pamela Dolan

Foreword by PETER H. RAVEN

Morehouse Publishing, 19 East 34th Street, New York, NY 10016
Morehouse Publishing is an imprint of Church Publishing Incorporated.

Cover image: KMNPhoto, iStock photo ID 503399218. Used with permission.
Cover design: Jennifer Kopec, 2Pug Design
Typeset by Newgen

Library of Congress Control Number: 2022930764

ISBN-13: 978-1-64065-540-9 (paperback)
ISBN-13: 978-1-64065-541-6 (ebook)

To my parents and stepparents, who taught me
to love words and gardens, and to strive for justice.
And to John, Annabel, and Kathleen,
with all my love and gratitude.

CONTENTS

Credit: Leslie Scoopmire

FOREWORD

The thousands of people who poured out into our parks and gardens following the tragic destruction that Americans experienced on September 11, 2001, were following strong instincts that have been with us since the very beginnings of humanity. We are all parts of a natural garden, one that includes all living things on Earth, and we feel most comfortable when we can figuratively reach back toward our origins. Among the principal ways we keep our place in nature visible are by maintaining areas of natural vegetation, by cultivating fields of trees or other plants, and by planting diverse gardens and parks around and near our homes and in our cities and towns.

Bringing to us in this book an important aspect of her life journey, Reverend Pamela Dolan inspires us and guides us toward finding our own inspiration. She gently leads us to consider taking time away from the demands of our busy lives to plant, tend, and harvest gardens and to enjoy the views of other gardens wherever we find them. In doing so, she helps us find the kind of quiet solitude that so many of us badly need today, much as we did after experiencing the horrible events of two decades ago.

Gardens and particularly gardening can certainly assist us in finding the internal peace that so often eludes us. They do so in part by leading us to experience the presence of a force greater than ourselves—that we are part of something larger. Whether we relate this force to our membership in the global web of life or extend it to a vision of a Creator, it is there, and we feel it. Whether we choose to grow flower gardens for our pleasure or vegetable gardens for our food, the pleasure of participating in the growth we witness is wonderful.

In the course of history, gardens have become regular parts of human lives. Our ancestors had to survive by constantly moving from place to place in an endless search for food, and because of that necessity, they were unable to develop permanent features of any kind. Some of these people migrated northward from Africa to Eurasia some 70,000 years ago; they soon spread east and southeast to China and Australia and, much later, west to the Americas. In central Eurasia, about 11,000 years ago, they made the most fundamental discovery in the life of humans on this planet—agriculture. They began to gather seeds from useful plants, planted and tended them, and settled down to enjoy the benefits of a secure supply of food year-round. When the first stages of this process were taking place, there were only about a million of us in the entire world—roughly the current population of Rhode Island! When they could simply remain in one place, however, producing the food they needed nearby, their numbers began to grow steadily. Starting with small villages at favorable sites, people began, over the course of time, to build larger and larger towns and eventually cities, so that the beginnings of what we know as the modern world became increasingly evident.

With all these developments, however, people very definitely remained a part of the living world, a world consisting of more than ten million other species of organisms. Although we shall always remain nothing more or less than one of these species, our influence on the global biosphere has come to dwarf that of all the others. The global ecosystem is comprised of a myriad of local ecosystems suited to the weather, soil, and other conditions of their own particular areas. While the great majority of other species inhabit just one of these areas, human beings have migrated widely, adapting to virtually every kind of local ecosystem in the process. Our collective influence today has spread worldwide, with drastic negative effects on the sustainability of the planet.

As our numbers have expanded, increasingly large numbers of other species have been subjected to a reduction in numbers or even disappeared completely from the face of the Earth. We really do not understand what the loss of so many species will mean to our own future, but we do know that we depend on them collectively and unavoidably as we push the limits of the world's carrying capacity. As contemporary religious leaders like Pope Paul and Patriarch Bartholomew I have consistently stressed, the loss of life poses a serious problem for us all, so that the extermination of that life should be considered morally unacceptable.

The earliest meaning of the word "garden," as in "the Garden of Eden," is a grove of useful trees and other plants—something that certainly would have been a benefit for the people living near it. In the pages of the *Epic of Gilgamesh,* which describes a period in Sumer nearly 5,000 years in the past, gardens are a feature. This is the earliest book that has survived to the present, and so we believe that such gardens likely date to the very beginnings of agriculture. More or less simultaneously, Chinese and Japanese gardens evolved in more formal directions, with Japanese gardens traditionally viewed as a kind of backdrop to life and Chinese gardens, formal to our taste, intended to command our attention.

Whatever their style and the nature of their origin, throughout history gardens have served as places for respite and meditation. They are where we are reminded, whether consciously or not, of our membership in the great community of life on Earth and of our compete dependency on other kinds of organisms. We are simply one of these many organisms; more than that, we could not exist without the others. In that sense, gardens remind us of our place in nature, described in such a meaningful way by Francis of Assisi nine centuries ago; in his "Canticle of the Sun," he wrote about "our sister Mother Earth, who feeds us and rules us, and produces various fruits with colored flowers and herbs."

European gardens, which continue to influence our gardens in the United States today, consisted primarily of useful plants with a selection of shrubs and trees to define their borders until the Renaissance, starting about five centuries ago, when innovations in every field were being fostered. People began to pay much more attention to the nuances and variety of nature, a trend illustrated remarkably by the beautiful woodcut prints of the German artist Albrecht Dürer. Columbus arrived in the Americas in the year of Dürer's twenty-first birthday (1492), his voyage marking a drastic change in the Europeans' perception of the world. With mounting imports of plants from America and particularly Asia, European gardens became increasingly diverse and varied. What had been demonstration gardens of medicinal plants at universities were developed into the botanical gardens of today, thousands of them, where anyone can learn about plants or participate in the development of the gardens themselves. Parks and garden-like cemeteries appeared as urban areas spread into the surrounding countryside and became important features of city life because of the values and insights that visitors derived from them.

In the pages of this charming book, Pamela Dolan has vividly portrayed the very personal parts of gardening, those parts that bring us and our contemporaries into close touch with seeds, with soil, with revival and rejuvenation, and with all the attributes that make us feel our connections to the living world. If we are believers, they also bring us in touch with our Creator, as they certainly do to the unseen forces that underlie the existence and functioning of the planet that we claim as our home. Nowhere more than by gardening and enjoying gardens and, beyond them, all of nature, can we appreciate more completely that we are part of a greater whole, one that comprises all life on Earth, and one that we continue to degrade and destroy at our peril.

One of the distinctive roles of gardens, which the Rev. Dolan discusses beautifully in chapter 5, brings into focus the world of humanity. While gardening, we may begin to realize that many people are not as fortunate as we who live in the wealthier parts of the world. If we have a large garden, why do others have none? Why have eight individuals accumulated as much wealth as the poorest 4 billion of us (out of an estimated 7.9 billion)? These are serious questions of social justice: overall, we are using far more than the Earth is capable of producing sustainably, while our population continues to grow rapidly and inequality becomes more pronounced with every passing year.

In conclusion, I can do no better than to invite each of you to journey with Rev. Dolan through the personal experience of gardening, to enjoy the gardens and parks of the world, and to find yourselves enriched as you pass along this way. You will find love, joy, and reverence as you marvel at the annual miracle of renewal in the familiar plants of your own garden. Bon voyage!

Peter H. Raven, President Emeritus,
Missouri Botanical Garden,
St. Louis, Missouri

Contemplative Gardening

The kiss of the sun for pardon, the song of the birds for mirth; one is nearer God's heart in a garden than anywhere else on earth.

—Dorothy Frances Gurney

INTRODUCTION

FINDING GOD BY DIGGING IN THE DIRT

Credit: iStock.com/cjp

"Nearer God's heart in a garden": The simple rhyme that serves as the epigraph to this book can be seen on signs and placards gracing countless garden beds. While it evokes the innocent charm of an earlier age, it also points to a profound and timeless truth: a garden is precisely where many of us experience the holy, whether we call that holiness "God" or "Creation" or just plain "nature."

This book is for anyone who wants to explore the connection between gardening and the divine. You don't have to be a good gardener, or even have a garden of your own. You don't have to be a person who follows a particular belief system; people of any faith or no professed faith can find spiritual solace and inspiration in a garden, if they're open to it.

It is no coincidence that popular interest in gardening is exploding at a time when people are hungry for hope and connection—to one another, to God, and to the earth. Mindful, spiritual gardening creates these connections and this necessary, life-giving hope. Gardens connect us to the past and to the future, although while we are working in a garden our minds are usually happily settled into the present moment. When you plant a seed and expect it to grow, you are following in the footsteps of countless others who have grown and tended that same species of plant, probably using many of the same tools and techniques that you will use. You are also exhibiting faith in the future, be it the expectation that you'll have delicious vegetables to eat in a few months or that generations yet unborn will enjoy the shade of the tree you are just now placing in your backyard.

Whether or not Martin Luther actually said it, there is great wisdom in the remark attributed to him: "If I knew the world were going to end tomorrow, today I would plant an apple tree." Our souls, our bodies, and our planet will all benefit from the committed care for creation that happens when gardening becomes a spiritual practice.

Definitions: Gardens and Gardening

Perhaps it sounds silly to define gardens and gardening, but for the sake of this book I want us to think of these terms in the broadest sense possible. As I have been writing, I've often paused to imagine a reader who lives in a small urban apartment. What could this book say to them? I hope it will have a great deal to say.

First, if you do not have access to a garden of your own, a place on land that you own or rent and can cultivate as you see fit, there is no need to despair. Many, perhaps most, towns and cities have community gardens where, for a fee, you get your own plot or raised bed and can grow what you like. If a community garden is out of reach (some do have long waiting lists or are too expensive), you might be able to find an organization that grows food for others and volunteer there. Many schools and faith communities have such gardens, and they usually welcome volunteers, including people from outside their organizations. These gardens can be a great way to learn from more experienced gardeners in an informal, low-pressure environment. Talking to people who teach gardening, through the Master Gardeners association in your area or a local community college or agricultural extension program, can also help you locate gardens that need volunteers.

If all else fails, you don't actually have to "garden" to reap some of the benefits of gardening that are discussed in this book. Just going out into gardens and parks and exploring them with the eyes of a contemplative gardener might be enough, at least as a start. Since I became a gardener, the character of my neighborhood walks has changed considerably. I now notice what other people are planting, get curious about why somebody is growing something well when my own similar specimen is struggling, and appreciate a well-designed front yard in ways I never did before. My own preference is more for growing fruits and vegetables than flowers, so I'm especially delighted when I see others utilizing edible landscaping in creative and clever ways. I learn a lot just by observing, but mostly it is my appreciation and enjoyment that have changed. Gardening has opened my eyes to the world around me. There is so much beauty and wonder in scenery that would have once struck me as ordinary and forgettable. This might be the greatest gift that gardening bestows—the ability to see the world in a new way, to fall in love with creation all over again.

Of course, you don't have to confine yourself to neighborhood walks if you want to engage in this kind of passive gardening, as I like to think of it. A city park, a botanical garden, or other well-landscaped public spaces can be equally inspiring, educational, and filled with delight. If you can get to a botanical garden or arboretum on a regular basis, do it, whether or not you are actively gardening elsewhere. These places are treasure troves of information and education, are often free or very low cost, and can be used for contemplative purposes as well. Repeated visits are especially useful; visiting during different seasons to observe how a garden or landscape is transformed by the onset of winter or the arrival of spring can help you feel even more in touch with the place, like getting to know a friend in different seasons of life. If this place is near where you live or work, consider just popping in for short visits as well as planning outings when you have more time to slow down and drink it in. When possible, go alone and keep distractions like music to a minimum—the idea is to focus on observation, on noticing both the world around you and your inner world with a bit more care and attention than usual on a walk or run that is primarily for exercise or other purposes.

The more gardens you visit, the more you will learn what appeals to you, and you can even begin to explore why that is. Some people just "click" with certain plants, and seeing that affinity as a gift and a doorway into your soul is a beautiful way to honor it. As I've said, I'm a basic vegetable gardener. I love watching plants grow, and do find aesthetic enjoyment in the different stages of a plant's life, but really in the back of my mind I'm always eager for the payoff, which is food. Harvesting blackberries or grape tomatoes and eating them while still standing out in the garden is a sublime joy to me, as is planning a meal around which veggies I know will be plentiful and ready to eat that day. But for other people, vegetable gardens are boring or too simple. Those people might gravitate to orchids, a great indoor plant, or rosebushes, or find their greatest joy in the design aspects of gardening, the shaping of a landscape over time. There is no right or wrong, no better

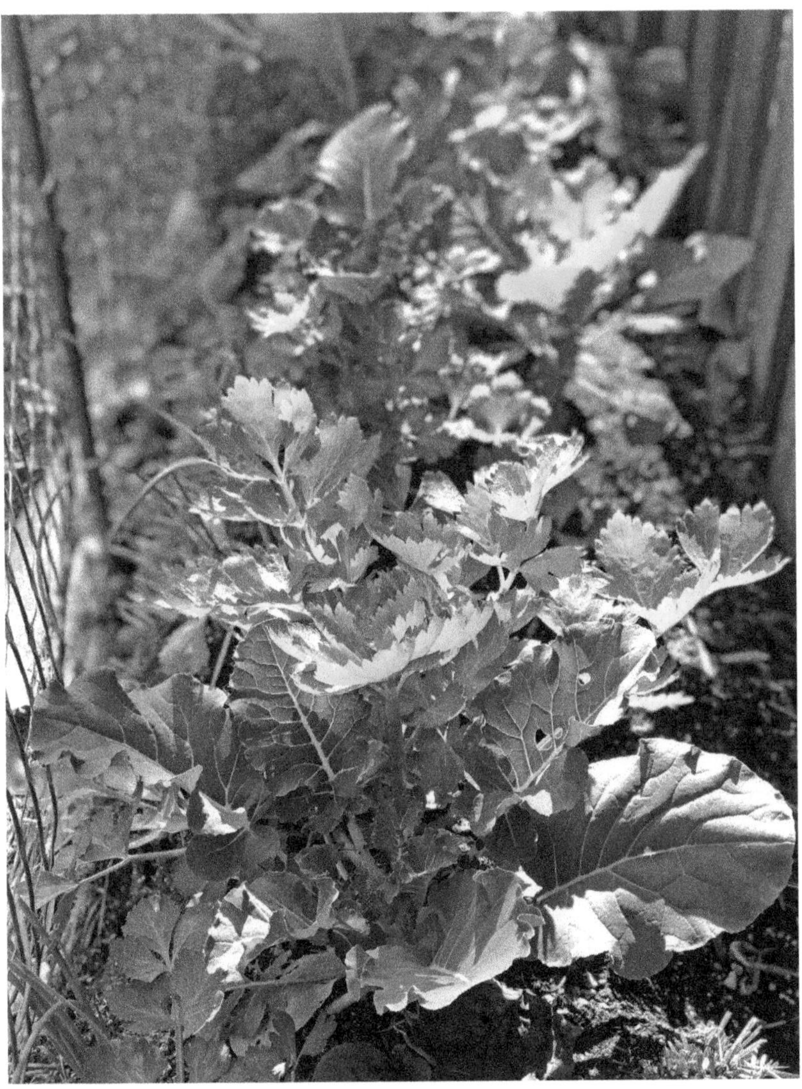

Winter vegetables in the author's straw-bale garden.

or worse, when it comes to garden preferences. Whatever you grow, or observe growing, can become a portal into a deeper understanding and appreciation for the divine spark of life that animates us all.

Finally, don't give up on growing things in your own space even if you don't have a lot of it. Houseplants are an option for nearly everyone. If you have any outdoor space at all, you can create a small container garden on a patio, deck, or balcony. It doesn't have to be an expensive endeavor: the internet is awash in great ideas about low-cost containers you can repurpose for growing plants. Good-quality, organic soil can be pricey, but for a small space you won't need that much of it and over time you might find better sources in your local community than the big-box home and garden stores. (Ooh, home and garden stores—yes, potentially full of temptations, but sometimes also great places for inspiration and appreciation.) Starting plants from seed is always less expensive than buying seedlings, although somewhat riskier for the beginning gardener. As you get to know other gardeners, they will often have cuttings or extra seedlings they are willing to share; gardeners are notoriously generous people.

Some of my favorite, unexpected ways to garden are methods I learned about online or from friends. Growing vegetables from scraps can be an amazingly fun project. Celery is the perfect plant for this; if you buy one whole bunch and cut off the end (obviously using the stalks for food), you can set it in water and watch it grow roots and sprout leaves, and soon you have your own new bunch of celery. YouTube is full of tutorials on how to regrow food from kitchen scraps: root vegetables, like potatoes and carrots, as well as onion, garlic, and many herbs can all be grown this way.

I'm also a huge fan of straw-bale gardening. This technique is a lifesaver in a small space or in situations where good soil is not available. When I moved into a new subdivision with no discernible topsoil to be found, I knew that straw-bale gardening would come to my rescue. The basic process is simple: You take a straw bale and prep it by adding organic fertilizer and water and making sure it gets plenty of sunlight. In a couple of weeks, the interior of the bale begins to heat up and decompose, creating a self-contained space for growing vegetables. I've had success with summer and winter crops, from broccoli to beefsteak tomatoes, and have been struck by what a useful option this can be for people with limited outdoor space. A straw bale is small enough to fit on most patios or balconies, or even in a parking space. It is also elevated, making it easier for people with back or knee issues, and tends to be almost completely weed-free (as long as you start with straw and not hay—hay bales will sprout and grow alfalfa or timothy hay or whatever they are made of, essentially becoming a large Chia Pet). The point is, with enough ingenuity and persistence, almost anyone, anywhere, can become a gardener.

Definitions: Spirituality and Spiritual Practices

Since every person you ask is likely to give you a slightly different spin on what spirituality means, I should probably offer my own best attempt at a definition. As a priest in the Episcopal Church, I find it easy to fall into "church-speak," that insider lingo that goes hand in hand with being part of a long-standing institution with its own rituals, routines, and vocabulary. By the way, gardening has its own insider lingo as well, much of it just as archaic and technical-sounding as anything the church goes in for. I'll try to avoid all that as much as possible in this book, or at least to provide definitions alongside the jargon when it happens that the jargony word really is the best I can do.

For me, *spirituality refers to an aspect of our inner lives that is both at the core of our being and that also exists beyond our individual selves, connecting us to God, one another, and all creation.* It's okay if you aren't crazy about the word "God"; you can certainly use terms like "Spirit" or "the Holy" to talk about essentially the same thing. Spirituality cuts across different faiths and belief systems; it's something innate and deeply human, which may or may not find an outlet in formal religious expression (consider the popularity of the label "spiritual but not religious").

A spiritual practice, then, is a discipline or habit that helps us cultivate depth and meaning in our spiritual lives; it is an activity that keeps our spiritual lives fresh, active, and growing. Obvious examples are individual prayer, reading Scripture, and participating in worship services. In the context of today's multifaith environment, practices like yoga, meditation, praying the rosary, and labyrinth walking are increasingly popular among all kinds of believers, and many people are discovering ways to turn simple, everyday activities, like knitting and coloring, into opportunities for contemplation and spiritual renewal and even for more focused, disciplined forms of prayer.[1]

To give an example from my own life, I once led a retreat for women where we talked about the feeding miracles in the Bible and then made bread together, in order to make the shift from a primarily intellectual apprehension of our faith to an intuitive, embodied understanding. With each ingredient we added to make the dough, we paused to tell a story about the spiritual significance of that item: water symbolizing new life, salt being a reminder of our unique giftedness, flour connecting us to a parable about the kingdom of God and a woman's reckless generosity, and so on. We used the time that it took for the dough to rise to share some of our feelings about how being female had shaped our relationship with God and with food, as well as with traditional notions of housework. We prayed while we kneaded the dough, allowing all our senses to be involved in the task, as the earthy smell of yeast filled us with feelings of hunger and anticipation. When the bread was almost ready, we began to celebrate a Eucharist together, pausing to sing as the freshly baked bread came out of the oven and cooled. One of the little loaves we had baked was blessed and used for communion, while the rest went home with the retreat participants.

Ever since that retreat, I have noticed an element of the sacred whispering around even routine baking and cooking tasks. Maybe it was there all along, and it took time with other women, the sharing of stories and songs and rituals, to bring it to my consciousness. Whatever triggered it, I now bake bread not simply to feed my family's physical hunger but also to feed something inside me that needs to be expressed physically. Baking bread, or really baking anything from scratch, is a whole-body experience, engaging all our senses. It is also a task that can lead to a flow state—if you've baked the same recipe many times, you can get into a kind of groove with it, simultaneously wrapped up in the steps of measuring, mixing, proofing, and so on, and also somehow utterly free and unencumbered.

Clearly, gardening fits into this category of spiritual practices that are based on the practical arts, crafts, or other ordinary activities—something simple and mundane, something people have done since time immemorial that, if performed with a certain level of awareness and intention, can become a spiritual practice. The goal of this book is to provide guidance along that path. How it actually plays out in practice will be different for every reader and every gardener.

Gardening is one of the most fundamentally human activities; people of all ages, abilities, and belief systems can adopt it as a spiritual practice. In this time of climate crisis, gardening is an important way to put our focus back on the earth, connecting us more deeply to nature's rhythms, the weather, water as a precious resource, and other elemental realities and thus making us better inhabitants of this planet we all share. Working in a garden reminds us that human existence depends on so much that is outside ourselves—we cannot single-handedly create soil, or make it rain, or cause a seed to germinate. Facing this reality is both humbling and uniquely grounding. At the same time, gardening gives us a sense of agency in regard to those outside forces that make our life possible. We can learn skills like composting, pruning, and setting up drip irrigation systems, competencies that are eminently practical and also help us feel like we are co-creating with the Creator, or at least participating in sustaining and nurturing creation. There is much soul satisfaction in these simple accomplishments.

Within my own tradition of Christianity, theologians Craig Dykstra and Dorothy C. Bass literally wrote the book on spiritual practices twenty years ago, and I cannot complete this introduction without acknowledging their profound influence on my thinking. They define spiritual practices as "*the human activities in and through which people cooperate with God in addressing the needs of one another and creation.*"[2] This definition is helpful in thinking about any kind of spiritual discipline, not only those practiced by Christians. It is something done, not just talked about; it meets one or more of the fundamental needs of humanity and creation; and it is responsive to God's presence in the world.

Let's consider briefly how this definition applies to gardening. To be sure, gardens address some of our fundamental needs. Gardens that grow vegetables and feed people obviously meet the human need for nourishing food, but other kinds of gardens are equally valid and meaningful, including ornamental gardens, medicinal or herbal gardens, memorial gardens, and prayer or meditation gardens. A garden with a purpose other than growing food will have a different impact on its community but can also be a source of profound healing and transformation; it can, for example, feed our human need for beauty, for respite, or for belonging.

Additionally, a garden can address a fundamental need and condition of all creation, not just of humanity, inasmuch as those who tend it choose to practice sustainable and environmentally friendly methods of gardening. Perhaps we gardeners should take the famous oath: First, do no harm. In growing our own food, especially, we can be part of a widespread movement that is seeking to address the myriad environmental and health concerns created by industrial agriculture.[3] We can prioritize care for creation over unrealistic productivity quotas and market competition. The fundamental need for all creation to be treated respectfully and as part of an interconnected web of life can be met by responsible and attentive gardeners. In this way both human needs and the needs of the land can be acknowledged and met by gardening when it is approached as a spiritual practice; we are truly cooperating with God, the one from whom all good things come.

Most of the examples of gardening I give in this book come from my own experience, and much of my gardening experience is a bit unusual in that it has been done in a community setting, specifically a church garden. There is no doubt in my mind that many people who garden alone in their backyards are gardening in a spiritual, mindful, even contemplative way. Most spiritual practices, though, do have a communal element. People who have a daily practice of centering prayer alone in their own homes, for example, may still meet with a centering prayer group weekly or monthly. I have friends who practice yoga and tai chi that way as well, balancing their individual practice with communal classes or gatherings. The point is, spiritual practices are intended to connect us beyond ourselves, rather than being solely about our unique and isolated relationship with the divine. Craig Dykstra helpfully calls spiritual practices "patterns of communal action that create openings in our lives where the grace, mercy, and presence of God may be made known to us and, through us, to others."[4] I would encourage anyone who wants to find more spiritual depth in their gardening life to consider adding some community gardening time to their routine. Being alone in a garden can be deeply restorative and meaningful as well, of course, but there is an added element to garden work done with others that creates that flow of energy, peace, and goodness that Dykstra is describing.

Finally, I like to remind myself that we use the word "practices" for a reason, and it is not about achieving perfection. Practices, like gardens, hold no guarantee of success. It is the doing of them, more than any measurable outcome, that makes the difference in our lives. In fact, Dykstra and Bass insist that practices are "always done imperfectly."[5] Gardens, too, have their inevitable imperfections and failures, no matter how much research and planning and hard work goes into them. My experience suggests that this is one of the primary lessons that gardens teach us: we are not in control, and the sooner we stop grasping for control and learn to work alongside creation the more joyful our time in the garden will be. As in so many other areas of life, it is often through our failures that we learn the most about gardening and ourselves, and find ways to be more creative and adaptive as time goes on. Gardens are an act of faith; as such, they teach us both to trust in the process and to hold lightly to the results.

What about Contemplation?

The term "contemplative gardening" is in some ways aspirational. To be clear, I don't mean by it that you will fall into a trance when you garden, achieving a "moment of Zen" so pure and electric that you transcend the normal limits of time and space. Or at least I can't say that anything like that has ever happened to me while gardening. Rather, *contemplative gardening is gardening that puts practice and process over results and accomplishment, focusing one's efforts on being in harmony with nature rather than achieving mastery over it.* Over time, it can and will lead to inner transformation, and that transformation should be felt throughout your life, not just while you are in a garden.

If I sound at all tentative about these claims, in part it is because I think the word "contemplation" is much misunderstood. Contemplation is not the same as ecstasy, which is an experience that takes you outside of yourself and even outside of any sense of being part of the material sphere. (The word "ecstasy" comes from the Greek roots *ek*, "out," and *histanai*, "to place or stand.") Contemplation, in contrast, always carries with it a sense of observation, of careful attention, and thus keeps us firmly in the physical sphere of reality. Its religious usage goes back to the early Middle Ages, and by the fourteenth century it had taken on the larger meaning of "holding an idea continuously before the mind."[6] In a more recent religious context, it is closely connected to a wordless and meditative type of prayer experience, like centering prayer.

The most trustworthy guide to the contemplative life I have ever encountered is Thomas Merton, the Trappist monk, theologian, social activist, and pioneer in the interfaith movement, who wrote more than fifty books before he died in 1968 at the age of fifty-three. He was, in a sense, a professional contemplative—nearly his entire adult life was lived in an enclosed monastery in Kentucky, where he practiced a life of prayer and silence. His writings on contemplation have shaped the way generations of would-be contemplatives understand the practice. In one of his most direct passages on the topic, he wrote:

> Contemplation is the highest expression of our intellectual and spiritual life. It is that life itself, fully awake, fully active, fully aware that it is alive. It is spiritual wonder. It is spontaneous awe at the sacredness of life, of being. It is gratitude for life, for awareness and for being. It is a vivid realization of the fact that life and being in us proceed from an invisible, transcendent and infinitely abundant source. Contemplation is, above all, awareness of the reality of that source.[7]

With that definition in mind, you can see why I might be careful about suggesting that gardening is synonymous with contemplation. At the same time, "spiritual wonder" and "spontaneous awe at the sacredness of life" are very apt descriptions of experiences

I have had while gardening, and "gratitude for life, for awareness and for being" seems a genuinely attainable, in fact likely, outcome of a regular practice of gardening mindfully and with intention.

This takes us back full circle to the definition of spiritual practices that considers them as responsive to God's presence in the world. Merton thinks of contemplation, too, as a kind of response; more precisely, "the response to a call: a call from him who has no voice, and yet who speaks in everything that is, and who, most of all, speaks in the depths of our own being."[8] Throughout history people in virtually every culture have heard something of this call in their encounters with nature. You see it in ancient Chinese landscape painting, the photography of Ansel Adams, the Romantic poets' outpourings, and innumerable other works of art and literature. This call is why people go to national parks, nature preserves, and other wilderness areas—we seek something there, something sublime and transformational, something that puts us in touch with ourselves as well as something beyond ourselves.

Gardening, in its humble way, does the same thing. While nothing as dramatic as a crashing ocean wave or a soaring mountain exists in a typical backyard garden, there are nonetheless opportunities for awe and wonder, even in something as gentle and delicate as the gradual unfurling of a leaf. "Start close in," the poet David Whyte advises, and it has always seemed to me that that is what contemplative gardening does: it invites us to start with the simplest materials, the most familiar tools, and the most easily learned actions, and then let the lessons unfold in due time. This kind of contemplation is rarely about a sudden, life-changing epiphany, although those *might* happen from time to time; instead, contemplative gardening works on our souls over the long haul, refining our awareness and unstopping our ears, making that still, small voice easier to hear and to respond to in gratitude and joy.

An Outline of What to Expect

Chapter One: Confessions of a Reluctant Gardener

This chapter tells the story of my own checkered history as a gardener, including the years I spent desperately avoiding yard work. The turning point came when I began a church vegetable garden as part of an effort to revitalize a small parish and make good use of our most valuable resource: land. We will also look at two Biblical creation myths and what they teach us about the interdependence of plants and people.

Chapter Two: Finding a Place

Finding a place to garden is a deeply grounding experience that can begin to ease the sense of "placelessness" that is part of modern life for most of us. This does not mean chucking everything and starting life over in a rural commune. This chapter will explore how any place where we choose to grow and tend plants can become a sacred place, and how the process of finding just the right spot will help put you in touch with the givens of the place where you live—the climate, the growing season, and other realities that our busy modern lives might otherwise lead us to ignore or misunderstand.

Chapter Three: Grounding Ourselves in Soil

Soil is alive. Without healthy topsoil, agriculture is impossible and the earth would no longer be fit for human existence—and yet how many of us think of dirt as a gift from God? After a brief foray into the science of soil we will consider the spiritual lessons it has to teach us. Soil is a metaphor for community; the underground mycorrhizal network of roots and fungi that lives in the soil is necessary for plant health, creating connections between different plants that allow them to communicate and cooperate. Similarly, our spiritual growth requires connection and communication to others; contrary to popular cultural myths, we do not succeed primarily through competition nor grow best in splendid isolation.

Chapter Four: Death and Compost

Gardeners are always looking for places with enough light—after all, plants need sunshine to grow. This chapter explores what might be seen as the "shadow side" of gardening. One of the great challenges and gifts of gardening is learning how little of what happens is in our control. Strangely, that most humble of gardening resources, compost, might be the greatest teacher when it comes to learning about cycles of life and death and new life, about how failure is always part of the process of creativity, and about how much of God's work in our lives happens in the dark.

Chapter Five: Hospitality and Justice

This chapter returns us to the themes of community and connection with which the book began, asking us all to consider ways that the garden can teach us about the ancient spiritual practice of hospitality and making room for others around the table. Contemplation can turn to action, hospitality to justice. Gardeners have an important role to play in building up beloved community.

What This Book Is Not

I am not a great gardener—or even a very good one. I say this without any coyness or false modesty. My mother is a Master Gardener, so I know what a good gardener is; my husband of twenty-seven years, meanwhile, does almost all the yard work. I work absurd hours as a parish priest and have little time for other pursuits; I probably read about gardening more than I actually spend time outside pruning and weeding. I am just as busy and distracted as all the people I counsel to become still and focused; I have a hard time keeping houseplants alive because I tend to get so absorbed in other things that I forget they're there.

So, why should you read a book *by me* about gardening? The only honest answer I can give is because I love it and because it has changed my life. That's what I'm really writing about in the pages that follow. I am not an expert; there are many, many other places where you can find solid, practical advice about gardening. Rather, I am someone who would like to come alongside others who are interested in this journey, others who also have an inkling that there is more to this gardening thing than meets the eye. If you are intrigued by the idea that digging in the dirt might be a pathway to God, if you've perhaps experienced a whisper of the divine while planting peonies or harvesting radishes, then we're already on this journey together.

CHAPTER ONE

CONFESSIONS OF A RELUCTANT GARDENER

My mother, everyone agrees, has a green thumb. Like many children, I was unaware of her talent while I was growing up—or at least unaware of how special it was. I suppose I assumed that everyone lived in a house that was filled with beauty, every inch of yard bursting with plants and flowers. Although we moved quite a bit, all our homes were like that. It only slowly dawned on me, I guess when I was old enough to begin spending time in friends' houses, that my mother's artistic ability—her eye—was a rare thing.

When I say my mother has a green thumb, I don't want you to get the wrong idea. Although my early years, spent in northern California in the 1970s, would have given her the perfect opportunity to be a laid-back hippie who grew medicinal herbs and talked to plants, she was not that. She was also not a sweet old lady who pottered around in her garden in a wide-brimmed hat, pulling up weeds by hand and sipping fresh lemonade on the porch in the afternoon. Had her own background been a bit different, my mom probably would have been an artist or an architect. Instead, she worked as an interior designer, and our homes were her showcase. Whether we lived on the outskirts of a small town in California or on the beach in Hawaii, any place we called home was always striking, somehow both inviting and a little glamorous, much like my mother herself. If you ever have the pleasure of meeting my mom at a cocktail party, she will probably strike you as a petite, stunning woman, elegant and refined, the perfect doctor's wife. Nothing about her screams earth mother or garden guru.

And yet, garden guru she is. Plants thrive under her care. Her yard always looks like it belongs in a glossy magazine spread—vibrant, brimming with color and texture in unexpected and pleasing combinations. And because she (mostly) doesn't hire landscapers or gardeners to do the work for her, as a child I spent a lot of time doing yard work. I mean *a lot* of time. It was what our family did on Saturdays and what many of my after-school chore lists were made of: watering, fertilizing, pruning, clipping, and so on.

Perhaps it was inevitable teenage rebellion that led me to dislike yard work so intensely. A therapist might refer to it as a time of necessary differentiation, an attempt to create an identity separate from my mother's, but whatever you call it, I began to balk at the hours spent outside, doing my admittedly rather small part in keeping our gorgeous yard looking tip-top. At some point in adolescence, I happily swapped those outdoor chores for inside ones—well, okay, maybe I wasn't exactly happy to wash windows or iron clothes, but it was better than getting all hot and sweaty and covered in grass clippings and dirt.

I wish I could say that I snapped out of this adolescent frame of mind as soon as I began to mature and have my own place to call home, but alas, I did not. I was, admittedly, an odd child. Although I grew up in places of extraordinary natural beauty, I longed for life in a city. Specifically, New York City. My imagination was captivated by the idea of living the life of a struggling writer—a "real artist"—which I had decided meant a life in an apartment, preferably sitting behind a typewriter, a cigarette smoldering nearby, coffee mug always at hand. Libraries, bookstores, university lecture halls—these were the places I wished to spend my days and my years. Sometimes these daydreams included the glitz and glamour that were sure to follow my artistic toil, including attending benefits and balls with a series of ravishingly handsome lovers. They never included any time out of doors, not even in a stroll through Central Park. The imaginary apartment life of my youthful dreams did not include a single plant.

It is funny to me to consider that that young girl is now a grown woman writing a book about gardening. And not just gardening but gardening as a spiritual practice. At the time I was both a devout Roman Catholic and also a quietly rebellious youth who assumed that some day I would grow out of my religious faith. My journey to who I am now has everything to do with faith, or serendipity, or the Force, or whatever you want to call that Thing that is bigger than we are and opens doors for us that we don't even know exist. It certainly has nothing to do with setting my own course and sticking to it.

For you see, I, who did not want to be a person of faith, who did not want to marry, who did not want to have children, and who definitely did not want to tend to a garden, am now an Episcopal priest, a wife, a mother, and a gardener. My daughters have grown up seeing me as that gardening guru or earth mother character I mockingly described earlier. I often wear a floppy hat and frequently talk to plants. I chose to move our family back to a small town in California, not far from where I lived as a child, so that we could be close to the University of California, Davis, the best agricultural learning center in the country, and be part of a community of people who know just about everything there is to know about plants and how to grow them. If I were to describe my dream home now, it would be an eco-friendly, solar-powered farmhouse, with plenty of room for goats and chickens and, of course, a garden overflowing with flowers and vegetables. What a long, strange trip it's been—and thanks be to God for it.

The Myth of the Green Thumb

Back to my mother's green thumb. I've sometimes thought it would be a good thing if we could eliminate that term from our vocabulary. The idea that some people have a green thumb and some people don't has caused far too many to despair of ever becoming a gardener, or even properly caring for their houseplants. So, why attach that label to my own mother?

As I've said, she has a talent for making plants grow and for arranging her garden in a pleasing, beautiful manner. Green and growing things do indeed thrive under her care. And therein lies the secret: care. The more time I've spent around other gardeners, and the more I've intentionally learned from my own mother (instead of running in the other direction when I see her pick up a garden hose), the more convinced I am that people with a green thumb are, by and large, just the people who take the best, most conscientious care of their plants.

Some may do this more intuitively, while others search out books and classes and YouTube videos for the information they need, but whatever it is that makes a good gardener, it's not magic. It is mostly work and time and attention. My mother is the perfect example of this. She lavishes time on her plants. When we had a large yard, my siblings and I became her landscaping crew, putting in hours of labor under her careful direction. But she always worked harder than any of us, often out watering and fertilizing and so on as soon as the sun rose. Behind the cozy illusion of a green thumb lay hours and hours of disciplined work.

It might not sound like it, but this is good news. If, like me, you got it into your head at some point that you aren't good with plants, maybe even that you're a plant killer, it is time to banish that thinking for good. Gardening can be learned—by anyone. I have seen tiny children and people well into their golden years tending to the same garden with the same joy and success. City kids who have only ever seen carrots that were first cut up and sold as "babies" in plastic packages can successfully grow and harvest vegetables without any special training. People with physical and mental disabilities can and do care for plants, often finding deep and abiding fulfillment in the process.

There are biological and evolutionary reasons for this. Despite how urbanized and technologized the world has become, virtually all human life on this planet depends on agriculture, on the ability to grow food. The fad of paleo diets notwithstanding, let's get real: there are very few true hunter-gatherer societies left, and certainly none in the industrialized West. There is also mounting evidence that the practice of growing food to supplement a hunter-gatherer's diet probably began well before the rise of farming, contradicting the old idea that agriculture was a response to food shortages that led to a completely different way of life—settled versus nomadic, and so on. This cultivation of occasional, supplemental food sources, something more scaled to feeding a household than farming tends to be, is what we would call gardening—and it doesn't surprise me in the least that it has been around for most of human history.

Although the practice of large-scale agricultural production, and certainly the development known as industrial agriculture, is a relatively recent human invention, cultivating plants for food is not. Even growing flowers simply because they're beautiful has been practiced by people for thousands and thousands of years. It is not a mere accident of etymology that the words "culture," "agriculture," and "cultivate" are all closely related—a culture, a civilization, is at heart a gathering of people who share common practices around growing, preparing, and eating food. Because gardening goes so far back in human history, it's not unusual to equate gardening with civilization itself. As Fred Bahnson, writer and permaculture gardener, puts it, "The garden is our oldest metaphor."[1] To create and maintain a garden, to cultivate land in an intentional manner, is to participate in a profoundly adaptive living tradition.

In the developed world, most people who garden do it for pleasure, not sustenance; many talented gardeners eschew edible plants completely and instead create entirely ornamental pieces of paradise. Gardens like theirs feed us, too, by nourishing our innate need for beauty and access to nature. Scientists are beginning to study the effects that green spaces have on our minds and bodies, and the findings are astonishing. That great American spokesperson for the benefits of time in nature, Henry David Thoreau, put it well in his classic *Walden*: "Shall I not have intelligence with the Earth? Am I not partly leaves and vegetable mold myself?" Well, yes. The truth at the heart of our existence is that we're all part of the earth, born to have "intelligence"—communication or even communion—with the soil from which we spring and on which all life depends. And

Credit: Leslie Scoopmire

gardening is one of the very best ways to encourage and enjoy that communion.

If nothing else convinces you that gardening is a core human activity, consider how pleasurable time spent in a garden can be. Even a humble vegetable garden stimulates all five senses. To my mind, the only readily available aesthetic parallel would be participation in truly high-quality liturgical worship, in that it is a whole-body experience with great spiritual import. At the height of its fruitfulness, a vegetable garden delights the eye with its countless shades of green and exclamation points of red, yellow, orange, and even purple. It provides tangible pleasure when you brush against soft leaves while walking between raised beds. It delights the ear (and the soul) primarily as a place of quiet, but not of total silence: in the hush of the garden you can hear droning bees and birdsong. Most especially it provides pleasure in the forms of taste and smell: the lingering aroma of a ripe tomato combined with the pungency of growing herbs; abundant edibles like sugar snap peas and the flowering stalks of bok choy that can be broken off and eaten without preparation while the sun warms your skin and the earth still steams from a recent rain.

So, no more worrying about who has a green thumb and who doesn't. Anyone can garden. You can garden. Take my word for it—if I can do it, you can, too.

Gopher Holes and the Garden of Eden

One of the first times I gave a presentation about my church garden, my mother was sitting in the first row of metal folding chairs that were lined up in a semicircle in a church basement classroom in Ketchum, Idaho. When I admitted that I had never been much into gardening while growing up, she laughed and reminded me of a story from my childhood. For years when I was very little my favorite thing to do was to play in the dirt and make mud pies. I would spend hours outside, collecting little twigs and rocks and leaves and stirring them up in an old metal bowl that my mom had allowed me to take from the kitchen.

Most days I sat under a big tree close to the house, finding all manner of organic goodies around the base of the tree and the nearby shrubbery. One day I wandered a bit farther, exploring my mother's vegetable garden. I'm not sure if I really remember any of this, or just remember the stories told about it later, but that first foray into gardening was not a great success.

I noticed that we had gopher holes around the yard, including quite close to the garden. Apparently, I got it into my head that I could get the gophers to come out of hiding (to what purpose I don't know—maybe I just thought they were cute?) if I used the hose to fill up their holes with water. Once I thought I'd put enough water into one hole and nothing happened, I moved on to another hole. My mother came outside eventually to find me in a sinking garden—I'd flooded so many holes with so much water that the entire garden was collapsing under me.

That's the kind of kid I was: curious, playful, and pretty clearly born without a shred of common sense. For as long as I can remember I've been called a daydreamer, a bookworm, a girl with her head in the clouds. It's no wonder that I found my identity wrapped up in cerebral pursuits, racking up academic awards and degrees. It would be many years before I would learn that many writers, readers, philosophers, and intellectuals of all stripes were and are also gardeners. The world is not as neatly divided into opposites as we like to think it is.

But there's another side to this story that I didn't see for a long time: I loved dirt. Our front yard, with its vegetable patch and walnut and olive trees, was a little bit of paradise to me. I was perfectly content to make my own fun and to let my imagination run wild for however long I was allowed to be outside. Besides making endless rounds of mud pies in an old mixing bowl my mom donated to the cause, I remember smooshing olives under my toes to see how dark the birthmark-like stain could get. I must have been filthy at the end of the day. When around age five I had to go to school (not a happy place for me at first), I would often spend recess alone on the edges of the playground, where dandelions grew in abundance and could become fodder for my imaginary worlds. Heaven was finally getting to walk home alone through the same fields where I harvested mustard flowers and other weeds, proudly offering these odiferous bouquets to my long-suffering family.

Even readers who aren't quite as quirky as I was might recognize a bit of themselves in the story of contented childhood hours spent unsupervised outside. It's astonishing how many memoirs I've read that share some version of that recurring pattern—childhood being a time for learning about the world and about ourselves by being outside, usually in close relationship with some particular spot, like the base of a big tree or the shady enclosure beneath a tall hedge. Some of the allure of gardening might even be that it allows us to escape back to the foundational pleasures of childhood, using our bodies and hands and imaginations in an outdoor space that becomes our own, not bound by any overt structure, external expectations, or the pressures to achieve and produce that are so much a part of adult life. I know I often experience a childlike sense of wonder and exuberance in the garden, and it's clear I'm not alone in that.

In the Beginning: The Garden of Eden

This theme of returning to the garden as a way to recover lost innocence is pervasive in our culture, and may find its source in a Bible story that is familiar not only to Christian and Jewish audiences but also to many who have no formal religious background at all: the Garden of Eden. At the beginning of the Bible, in the first chapter of the book of Genesis, readers learn of two creation stories. One is the familiar seven-days narrative, with creation unfolding in an orderly fashion, a series of separations (light from dark, water from dry land, and so on) and of makings ex nihilo, from nothing. In this first creation myth, God makes plants, animals, and all of what we would now call "nature"—including human beings—through a series of utterances. God doesn't need to *do* anything except speak for things to come into existence and then be proclaimed good. At the end of the sixth day, God explains that all the plants and trees have been given to the people and to the animals for food, and then proclaims it all *very good*. The repetitive structure of this myth makes it easy to remember, at least in broad outline, and suggests that it likely was used for liturgical or ritual purposes.

A second creation story occurs in the next chapter of Genesis, and it is there that we encounter the Garden of Eden. Interestingly, and in a blow to people who try to read the Bible literally, the order of creation is roughly reversed in this story. In this version, we start not with a void but with a land already formed, covered with a mist that was "going up from the land and was watering the whole face of the ground" (Genesis 2:6). There is no mention of where this land came from, or who made it or the mist. They are simply givens, a starting point, or perhaps the key ingredients needed before God can make everything else. The story does tell us explicitly that it takes place before God had made plants, and it links the creation of plants to two things: rain and people. Plants were only possible because of the existence of rain to water the earth and people to "work the ground."

God, however, gets to work right away, seemingly creating both humankind and rivers with the express purpose of making plant life possible. That very first person, not yet named, is formed from the "dust of the ground" and God's spirit breathed into his nostrils. This fashioning of humanity from base materials is markedly different from the process of speaking into existence that occurs in the first creation myth. People seem more embodied in this version, and much more connected to the other forms of life that are soon to spring into being. As soon as God creates that first person, God places him in a garden, a garden soon filled with "every tree that is pleasant to the sight and good for food." And then God quickly moves on to creating a river that flows from the garden and into the four regions of the known world.

In this second creation myth, in other words, the garden is the source of all life that comes after it. Note that the garden is "in Eden, in the east," likely connected to the rising of the sun and the renewal of life that accompanies it. The garden is also the thing that gives humanity purpose: "The Lord God took the man and put him in the garden of Eden to work it and keep it" (Genesis 2:15). This is as clear a statement of why God made people as any we will find in the Bible, one that ought to provide a blueprint for adherents of all three Abrahamic faiths when thinking about the meaning of life and our ultimate purpose. We are here because we are a part of the earth, created by God to care for it.

Scholars have written extensively about what the Hebrew words that we translate as "work" and "keep" really mean.[2] I won't rehash all the arguments, but suffice it to say that these verbs are used here with a strong connotation of care and attention. This foundational myth is not pointing to a hierarchical relationship between people and the rest of creation, let alone a utilitarian or crassly economic one. Put simply, the world does not exist for us to dominate it, extract all we can from it, or make money from it. Nor do we exist only to produce, consume, achieve, or compete. The primary human mode is one of tending and caring, as much for men as for women. Creativity, connectivity, and reciprocity are all implied. Our tending helps plants thrive, and in turn they provide us with the nourishment we need to thrive as well.

If some people are able to read a sense of hierarchy into the first creation myth—believing that people are made on the penultimate day of the week because we are the pinnacle of creation, somehow closest to God—this version of the story offers a radical leveling of that hierarchy. Our being first in the order of creation does not imply anything about our worthiness or relative importance but rather connotes that we are an essential piece of the puzzle. Human beings aren't made of better stuff or for a separate purpose from the rest of creation. Both human and plant life have the same source: God, yes, but God working through the soil. God creates the first human (Adam) by pulling him out of the earth (*adamah*), much the same way that God pulls out all the plants, the trees, and indeed the water needed to sustain life. The implication is clear: since we are all made out of the same stuff and have the same maker we must be deeply connected, even in an important sense related. This interconnectedness gives shape and meaning to our lives. Plants and herbs were not created until after a human being was made who could care for them; conversely, there are attributes of plant life that make sense only if people exist to see them and take nourishment from them. This is the beginning of community as a kind of benign, even productive symbiosis—plants need people to fulfill their purpose, even as people need plants both to use and enjoy.

For me this story is both humbling and deeply liberating. I don't come from a religious tradition that teaches people to read Scripture literally, so I have never had to figure out how to square so-called creationism with the scientific theory of evolution. Nor do I feel any need to force the two different creation myths presented in Genesis into some kind of rigid agreement with each other. Nonetheless, these stories have profoundly influenced how I see the world. I have spent much of my adult life reading and rereading them, learning from others who are more familiar with the cultures, history, and language that shaped them.

The story of how God made the world in seven days reminds me that all of us are made in God's image, male and female, and that this truth is more important than any other label we might choose to attach to groups or individuals. We are all radically loved and cherished by the greatest force in the universe—and so is everything else in nature. Everything that God made God then proclaimed to be good, so treating it all with love and respect is not optional for people of faith. God loves light and darkness, rain and dry land, earthworms and elephants and eggplants, and so I should love them all, too.

The second creation myth, meanwhile, grounds me even more deeply in my sense of createdness, or creatureliness. (These words are not recognized by spellcheck, but I hope they might resonate with anyone who has read this far.) Not only am I just as "good" and loved as all of creation, but we are all made from the same stuff and are inextricably linked. I am part of a web of earthly existence, dependent on other forms of life, some of which also depend on me. These insights inform not only my faith but also my daily life choices. I am training myself to remember that what I do has ripple effects throughout society and the natural world, from what I eat to where I shop, from how much I recycle and compost to what clothes I wear and for how long I keep them out of the landfill. These are not simply "lifestyle choices" but ethical decisions with far-reaching effects, most of which I will never see directly.

Contemporary science backs up this view of life as an interdependent web of being. Darwin wrote about an "entangled bank" as a metaphor for the natural world he sought so faithfully to understand. Because his insights about evolution are often simplistically boiled down to phrases like "survival of the fittest," his more nuanced understanding of how interconnected all of life is can be lost in the popular imagination. Many biologists, botanists, and others working on environmental issues are reclaiming the central role that cooperation and collaboration have in our ecosystems, illustrating in one beautiful, surprising example after another that competition is not the exclusive or even primary mode of relationship in nature. We'll look more closely at these insights when we talk about community in Chapter Three.

What strikes me now, writing about these origin stories, is that the Western world's religious imagination could have been shaped by the foundational insight that we are all created for the purpose of tending to the land—in other words, that gardening is the original human vocation. Instead, these stories were quickly put to different uses, becoming spiritualized and moralized, so they were thought to be about abstract concepts like original sin or the pseudoscience of creationism. The idea that God made people for the explicit purpose of caring for the land went underground, so to speak, and when it was articulated by various Christians throughout the centuries it was often dismissed as fanciful, fringe thinking, mistaken for paganism or pantheism, or even condemned as heresy. I wonder how different the whole history of Western civilization would be if these myths had been taken more seriously as blueprints for how we were to live in the world, as partners and co-creators rather than as conquerors, colonizers, and controllers.

Paradise Lost, Paradise Found: Recovering Our Original Vocation

A related universal truth embedded in the Garden of Eden story is the reality of separation from the earth, poignantly narrated as banishment from the garden. Once again, even people who have never read the Bible itself probably have gleaned some general cultural knowledge of a story about an apple, a serpent, a woman, and other elements of what is usually called the Fall. However you understand this story, whether it is about disobedience or overreaching or some other violation of boundaries, the consequences of it are crushingly relevant to human history and the situation in which we find ourselves today. In Genesis 3, God's punishment extends first to the serpent and then to Eve, burdening them with enmity and pain; only after dealing with them does God turn to Adam with these words: "Cursed is the ground because of you; in toil you shall eat of it all the days of your life; thorns and thistles it shall bring forth for you; and you shall eat the plants of the field" (Genesis 3:7–18). Finally, God banishes the couple from the Garden, sending them into eternal exile.

Exile from the garden would seem to be a sadly apt metaphor for where we are as a species today. Most of us in the modern Western world do not have a close relationship with the land on which we live, work, worship, and play. We don't know much about growing things, where our food comes from, or what our soil is made of; this kind of knowledge, once passed along from generation to generation, is now seen as the purview of specialists, rather than as essential, commonsense know-how.

Many people of faith, as well as climate scientists and environmentalists, have begun drawing lines of causation from this separation or dislocation to the ravages of climate change. The heartbreaking reality is that most of us who live in countries that are having the biggest impact on the planet simply don't know enough about the land to know how to love it and care for it properly. We don't see the connection between our lifestyle, our overconsumption, our waste, and the harms that the planet is suffering because of them. We have lost a sense of our original vocation as people created to care for the earth, and the results have been catastrophic.

It may sound preposterous, but for many of us the simple practice of gardening can be the key to reversing our exile from creation. I believe this to be true based on my own life experience, as well as the difference I have seen gardening make in the lives of others.

As I mentioned earlier, as a child I loved playing in the dirt. But as soon as yard work became a chore on my to-do list, I rebelled. Adam and Eve had nothing on me. By the time I was in college—having chosen a big urban university over a prestigious college in a leafy suburb of Boston because to me "the city" was synonymous with intellectual sophistication—I had no interest whatsoever in soil, science, plants, or the natural world. I had bought in completely to the myth of separation: mind from body, nature from soul, the physical world from the spiritual one. I was in exile, and I didn't even know it.

It was a garden that returned me to myself.

This particular garden came into my life when I was a few years into my chosen profession, one I had come to in midlife;

I was ordained a priest at the age of forty-two and, in the lingo of the Episcopal Church, was called to be the rector of a parish a couple of years later. This parish, located in a wealthy white suburb of St. Louis, was small and, in many ways, struggling. The struggles were similar to what so many religious organizations are going through these days: declining membership, an aging congregation, internal conflicts, and on and on.

Through a process of discernment, we realized that one of the greatest assets we had was land; the church sat on five acres of lovely, open space, most of it unused and covered in lawn. The congregation was proud of this peaceful, parklike setting, but for six days of the week much of it sat empty, except for the occasional neighborhood kid kicking around a soccer ball or playing catch with her dad. The question that began to capture my attention was how best to make use of the land so that it worked for the church in a generative way, whether financially or in terms of social capital, new energy, connection with the surrounding community, or even something else that we could not yet see.

When plans to sell off part of the property and use the money for revitalization efforts failed, we got more serious about the work of communal discernment. Many ideas were floated, discussed, and discarded. Ultimately, we settled on building a garden, growing vegetables, and giving away the produce to people in need. It sounded simple enough.

There was nothing simple about starting a church garden, as it turned out. Change is always hard, even harder in church, and perhaps hardest of all for churches that feel threatened or stressed. Instigating change can feel like accepting criticism; the way we have been doing things must be wrong or bad, or else why would we need to do something different? But often change is necessary not because the old ways were wrong or bad but because circumstances have changed, the world has changed, and the old ways simply no longer serve us.

The property at my midwestern parish was a case in point. It was designed during a time when the cultural zeitgeist was all in the direction of conformity. The landscaping was perfectly appropriate for the 1950s church, when the institution was assumed to be a secure part of the fabric of American society. The acres of rolling green lawn, with the discreet brick building of the church tucked away well off the main road, fit in with the surrounding aesthetic at a time when fitting in, being part of the establishment, was what mainline American Christianity was all about. Nearly six decades later, the cultural and religious landscape had changed dramatically, but the church's physical property appeared to be stuck in a time warp.

To the passerby, there was nothing to see that spoke of our theological commitments, no embodiment of the doctrine of creation. Our grounds did not celebrate nature, as might have been achieved using prairie grass or other indigenous plants for landscaping, nor did they celebrate anything distinctive about Christian culture or beliefs by being beautiful or useful. In the Book of Common Prayer we pray, "O heavenly Father, who has filled the world with beauty: Open our eyes to behold your gracious hand in all your work; that, rejoicing in your whole creation, we may learn to serve you with gladness."[3] Church architecture and landscaping should serve as aesthetic and sensory aids to help open people's eyes, to make it easier to see beauty and from beauty to see God's love and creativity at work. The layout of our grounds, with its unmitigated expanse of lawn, made us appear neutral, in the sense of being essentially the same as any other building in the neighborhood, from a post office to a house to a school. It certainly in no way hinted that what we were offering inside our doors was transformation, true fellowship, and the way of life abundant.

While that all seemed obvious to me, with my fancy theological education and my grand visions and plans, it was a surprise to many parishioners who were perfectly happy with the way the church looked and felt. Some were unsettled by the idea of using part of the land for a garden. At the time, this felt to me like simple resistance to change. In retrospect, I can see that those parishioners were not wrong to sense that starting a garden would have major ripple effects.

In March 2014, we broke ground for the garden, which we dubbed Shepherd Farm. We chose a thirty-by-ninety-foot plot on the far side of the church building, visible from the road but not taking too much out of our five-acre property, surrounded it with a deer fence, and got to work. Eight to ten core volunteers gardened regularly throughout the spring, summer, and fall. It was not a big group, but it was a significant percentage of the parish: our average Sunday attendance that year was sixty-five. According to the volunteer logbook we kept on hand, forty or so people spent at least one hour each in the garden at some point during the season. By the end of October, we had harvested 2,083 pounds of food, almost all of which was delivered to various hunger ministries. In our second season, despite more challenging weather conditions, we harvested slightly more: another 2,107 pounds of produce, also for the benefit of those in our area who were food insecure or downright hungry.

Those numbers tell a story, but I hope you can imagine by now that the story of the garden is much bigger than even those numbers would suggest. My intentions in starting the garden had to do with growing our community and feeding the hungry.

Those intentions were present throughout my involvement with Shepherd Farm—they are evergreen needs, sufficient and meaningful in and of themselves. But for me as a human being and a person of faith, the impact of the garden was far bigger than anything I could have imagined when it began. Terms like "creation care" and "eco-spirituality" sound so abstract, so idealized and remote from everyday life. The Shepherd Farm garden was the opposite of abstract or remote. It changed my life, expanded my horizons, shifted the focus of my ministry, and saved my soul. That's a lot for a thirty-by-ninety-foot plot of earth to accomplish in just a couple of years.

The lessons I learned from that garden, the way it saved me by returning me to myself, will be much of what I share in the rest of the book. I'll conclude this chapter with just one example of a spiritual gift from the garden: beginner's mind.

Beginner's Mind: The First Gift of the Garden

One of the great things about learning something new in midlife is that it puts us back in the mindset of a beginner, giving even the most mundane realities a sheen of wonder. There were challenges in learning gardening the way I did; it was, in a very good way, a most humbling experience. Before I became a priest, I was trained as an academic, where knowledge, skill, and expertise are highly valued. Now I was also in charge of a congregation, a position that often feels like it comes with the expectation of having all the answers. And yet I was a brand-new gardener, learning daily from parishioners who had vastly more knowledge than I.

At first, I worried about every little thing I did in the garden, as if the entire garden's well-being were on my shoulders.

But over time I learned that my watering, weeding, and pruning only had to be good enough, not perfect, for the plants to thrive.

I also had to learn that I could only truly learn something new by getting comfortable with my own ignorance. Asking silly questions, needing someone to show me repeatedly how to tie up a vine or explain how far apart the seeds should be planted—this felt embarrassing at first, like there was so much I *should* know that I didn't. It was important to move past that feeling if I didn't want my own ego to get in the way of the goal, which was to grow food for people who needed it. Keeping that goal in mind was what motivated me to get over myself and enjoy learning something new.

That first summer of gardening, our beds of cherry tomatoes practically exploded with fruit. There were more tomatoes than we could possibly keep up with. I'd go out in the evening to harvest everything I could and then the next morning would find the ground littered with tomatoes that somehow, in those intervening hours, had become overripe and simply fallen off the vine. Sometimes the ones on the ground could be harvested, but often they were already being eaten by bugs and other critters. There was something bordering on the obscene about all that ripe fruit scattered everywhere, bursting with seeds and the aroma of summer. I found myself frustrated that I couldn't keep up and was haunted by the sense that we were wasting food that could have gone to the hungry.

The next spring, we planted that same bed with brassicas—cabbage and cauliflower and such. One day I was weeding in that area and almost pulled up a tall, gangly interloper before I noticed that it looked familiar. On more careful inspection,

I realized that we had a bunch of tomato plants growing in among our leafy greens.

Puzzled, I asked one of the experienced gardeners if she had planted tomatoes there and, if so, how we were planning to stake them. She managed not to laugh as she walked me back to the bed and pointed out what was happening. These tomato plants, she gently explained, were "volunteers"—nobody had intentionally planted them there. They were just growing of their own accord, undoubtedly the result of seeds that had fallen to the ground the season before.

Then it hit me—the fallen tomatoes I had worried so much about in August hadn't been wasted at all. Many had fed our nonhuman neighbors, likely including some that were quite beneficial to our ecosystem. Others had left their seeds behind, unseen and untended, and now we had a whole new crop of tomato plants and could begin the cycle anew.

To an experienced gardener, finding a bunch of volunteer tomatoes would be about the most unexceptional experience imaginable. For my beginner's mind, though, it was a revelation. Who knew that tomatoes could just set up house like that all by themselves, unaided by human hands? It was like they had a mind of their own.

I am grateful that I had kind and generous teachers; their attitude allowed me not to hide my ignorance but to approach the garden with curiosity and an eagerness to learn. That spring day, in addition to learning about volunteers, I also gained a whole new appreciation for how little of what happens in a garden, or in life, is in my control, and how much of it I really just need to hand over to God. This is beginner's mind, the perspective that finds cause for delight and wonder in the most ordinary of events. Some people call this experience "seeing with fresh eyes."

I would imagine that most people who have heard about beginner's mind associate it with Eastern practices like yoga and meditation. But I believe it is an essential building block for any form of spiritual practice. Without it, the resistance we have built up as adults to looking foolish or doing something incorrectly—in other words, to learning—is a constant impediment to growth, making everything more difficult than it needs to be.

One of the ways that my own religious tradition encourages the development of beginner's mind is through parables. In the New Testament books we call the Gospels, Jesus does most of his teaching in parables. These are stories that don't make immediate sense, in which the normal rules of everyday life don't apply. Although short, they often contain memorable characters and humorous levels of hyperbole, and they always set about to upend our expectations and leave us wondering about what they mean. Unlike a fable or a story with a neat moral, a parable should actually cause us to doubt what we know, or what we think we know, at least for a moment. In addition, many of the parables are horticultural or agricultural in theme—in other words, they take place in a garden or farming context and are about growing things. I doubt this is coincidental.

To use a well-known example, let's take a look at a parable from the Gospel of Mark, commonly referred to as the parable of the sower. In it a farmer scatters seeds on four different types of ground, each yielding a different result. This appears to be done not in a methodical, scientific way but instead rather haphazardly and even carelessly. Not surprisingly, most of the seeds do not thrive. The seed scattered on a path gets eaten by birds.

The seed that lands on rocky places doesn't have enough soil to grow deep roots, so it grows quickly but just as quickly withers and dies. The third scattering of seeds lands in a patch of thorns, and the weeds choke the plants that the farmer is trying to grow. Finally, there is seed that "fell on good soil" and grows into a successful, bountiful crop.

Most sermons and commentaries on this story focus on the different places where the seeds landed and ask the audience to draw parallels between these places and different states of mind or soul—what it takes to be "good soil" for God's word instead of a rocky place or a patch of thorns, and so forth. Occasionally someone will note the absurdity of a farmer who doesn't seem to know what conditions his seeds need for growth, including the most basic component of farming, which is to have decent soil. I think this is an important clue to an aspect of the parable that is often overlooked. To be clear, this is definitely not a story about a poor benighted peasant from two millennia ago who didn't understand basic botany. We need to remember that the average person two thousand years ago likely had a great deal more practical agricultural knowledge than the average American today, given that most people then lived and died by their ability to grow and harvest food successfully.

Remembering the agrarian context in which Jesus lived and taught, we ought to consider that the farmer's cluelessness matters, that it isn't in the story by accident. Perhaps it is meant to catch our attention, to make a point. It's certainly not meant to be an example for us to follow literally when it comes to growing food—there's no virtue in wasting resources in a garden or not doing your homework about the best conditions for growing your preferred crop. Still, this seemingly clueless farmer actually might be a paragon of *spiritual* virtue, of faith in the sense of trusting in God's providence. As a farmer, he's a failure. But as an allegory for beginner's mind, he is spot on. Beginner's mind, something a little like innocence or openness, cannot thrive in an environment that is overly calculated or where success is guaranteed. It is a doorway to spiritual growth that is easily cultivated in a garden.

The parable that comes directly after this one in Mark's Gospel is also agrarian and also illustrates the importance of beginner's mind. Like its subject matter, the parable of the mustard seed is notable for how small it is—only three verses long. It is short enough to quote in full here:

> Jesus also said, "With what can we compare the kingdom of God, or what parable will we use for it? It is like a mustard seed, which, when sown upon the ground, is the smallest of all the seeds on earth; yet when it is sown it grows up and becomes the greatest of all shrubs, and puts forth large branches, so that the birds of the air can make nests in its shade." (Mark 4:30–32)

Where I live in northern California mustard grows wild—the fields around my hometown turn vivid yellow with the large flowery bushes early in the spring, as long as we've had enough winter rain. It can grow quite tall but is nothing like a tree with large branches, nor is it likely to be called "the greatest of all shrubs." That, though, is not the kind of mustard plant referenced in Scripture. Rather, this is likely African mustard, which grows in the Middle East even in very arid conditions. Like the plant in the parable, it starts with a small seed and becomes a large bush, tall enough to be considered a tree.

People often say that this parable refers to the spread of Christianity, from a tiny, humble beginning in Galilee to a worldwide religion that has changed the course of history. With all due respect to generations of preachers, that's just silly. Jesus is not talking about Christianity, which developed in the generations after his death. He's nudging us to adopt a mindset that sees potential for growth and transformation in even the unlikeliest of places. We don't need to overthink this. Just imagine a child who puts a small seed into a plastic cup full of dirt and watches in awe on that day when a little shoot pops up from the dirt and becomes a bean plant. That's what Jesus is asking of us—not just the faith to believe that such a thing can happen but the humility to accept that when it happens it has much more to do with God than with us, and the openness to be awed by it, no matter what our age.

In thinking about this parable, it occurred to me that if a committee of experts got together with the express purpose of creating an enormous bush that could provide shade and food for birds and animals in the desert, they would never reverse-engineer a mustard seed. That's the miracle of growing things that we forget or ignore if we don't have beginner's mind. Not only mustard seeds but most seeds are so unassuming, so ordinary. To the untrained eye they don't look any more alive than a pebble. And yet what a life force lives inside them, what a world of vitality just waiting to be born.

I am grateful that I can experience this beginner's mind in the garden, as when I was flabbergasted with delight at the appearance of volunteer tomatoes. And yet I am woefully aware that I don't always carry this gift with me everywhere I go outside the garden gates. It is so easy to slip back into other ways of seeing and behaving, to lose that openness and curiosity and wonder.

Discussion Questions

1. What are your earliest memories of or connections to gardening?
2. What does it mean to see ourselves as a part of creation?
3. What has to change in our lives to live in better relationship to other living things?
4. What is the ongoing value of being a beginner?

CHAPTER TWO

FINDING A PLACE

Location, location, location. We've all heard that it's the only thing that matters when it comes to real estate, but the same is mostly true of gardening as well. Figuring out the "where" of your garden is a key component of its success. That said, many of us will not have a lot of choice when it comes to where we can grow things. If you are a homeowner, it's unlikely you were able to choose your home based on the quality of the soil, the amount of sunlight in the backyard, or similar garden-friendly considerations. You might feel even less empowered if you rent your house or apartment; perhaps you don't have a yard, or you don't have permission to do much with it if you do.

This is where gardeners need to get creative, and creativity begins with curiosity. Getting to know your space is essential. Assuming you have some outdoor space, even if it's a small balcony, you need to become aware of its essentials, like how much sunlight it gets in a day and how exposed it is to the elements—if it tends to be very windy there, if the sun beats down on it relentlessly in summer, and so on. You need to think about where the closest source of water is, assuming you're not somewhere that gets so much rain you don't have to worry about that. If you're looking at an outdoor space, you'll want to learn about the type of soil you have, and how it may need to be enriched or amended. In a sense, you need to start thinking like a plant, or at least thinking about a plant's needs, as you scout out locations. Luckily, you'll find that almost any location can meet some plant's requirements; the trick is to match the plant to the space.

When we talk about the fundamentals of a location—like soil type, amount of sunshine and rain, and so forth—we are talking about a place's *givens*, its reality. Contrary to some popular myths that see spirituality as almost the opposite of practicality, the spiritual life is as dependent on the givens of life as gardening is. This idea might take some getting used to, especially if your image of a spiritual person is a yogi or mystic tucked away in a remote monastery, cut off from the so-called real world. While I agree that mystics, monastics, and yogis all have a lot to teach us about spirituality, I would also argue that they are not really any less involved in "the real world" than the rest of us. In fact, those images of spiritual masters in their special set-apart places might actually help us recognize that, when it comes to our spiritual lives, location matters.

If it's true that people going through intensive spiritual training do usually choose to set themselves apart in places that help cultivate the habits of life and mind they are seeking to develop, that might be precisely *because* our context and surroundings have a strong influence on our interior lives. Places matter. Even for the rest of us, the regular folks, it's entirely normal to find some settings more conducive to prayer, meditation, and general mindfulness than others. Places of worship are designed with this in mind. If you are someone who prays, you probably already know that the quality of your prayers, the feel of them, can be influenced by the type of building you're in, or whether you're in a building at all.

Places of Prayer

Let me give a couple of examples from my own life. During college, I spent a lot of time in church. I went to an entirely secular public school, the University of California at Berkeley, so going to church was a personal choice that started during the first days of my freshman year. I was far from home and grieving the unexpected death of a close friend, and church became a refuge and a place of comfort. The campus ministry for Catholic students at UC Berkeley is housed in the same building as the parish congregation. It's a stark, modern, fortress-like structure; there are few statues, icons, or other liturgical decorations to soften the space. Some people find it cold and a bit forbidding. Week after week, though, I worshiped there at ten o'clock on Sunday nights, the entire nave filled with flickering candles and the sound of gentle guitar music. During those late-night masses, my whole mind would become focused on the words of Scripture and the sound of the hymns; there was very little to see in the near-darkness, so my other senses took over and many of my thoughts and prayers went inward, deep down into the recesses of my soul. It was a healing balm to everything that ailed me.

By contrast, All Saints' Chapel in Sewanee, Tennessee, is an enormous, light-filled Gothic Revival church absolutely chock-full of jewel-toned stained glass, splendid banners, and lavish ornamentation. I have worshiped and prayed there many times, and the whole impression is utterly different from what I experienced in Berkeley. When I'm in All Saints' Chapel I don't want to close my eyes; instead I find myself basking in all the visual glory of the place. My prayers there tend to be more outward-focused, more heavenward, I suppose. I feel stimulated rather than grounded, like I want to fly out of there and straight into the arms of God. Some of the difference in my experience of these two worship sites is personal to me and has to do with my own context and circumstances. But much of it is a result of the places themselves, of their different characters and styles.

These two contrasting states I've described line up roughly with what classic studies of spirituality would call immanence and transcendence. *Immanence* means that the experience is more immediate, embodied, and inward-focused. The word itself comes from the Latin for "to dwell or abide." *Transcendent* experiences, as the name implies, take us out of ourselves, into an otherworldly or even out-of-body state. The Latin roots for this word mean "to climb beyond." One of the most helpful ways I've heard to understand these two states of mind is to think of them as forming a cross. Immanence aligns with the horizontal axis, encompassing everything on this plane of reality, while transcendence aligns with the vertical axis, pushing up and away, toward the heavens.

In the West, and especially in the United States, we tend to see these two planes as entirely separate and distinct, and in fact quite opposed to each other. The horizontal axis is simplified and reduced to the material world, while the vertical axis becomes all about spirituality, as if spirituality and transcendence were synonymous. This both elevates the idea of spirituality and, paradoxically, diminishes it. Think about that image of the yogi on the mountaintop or the monk in his cell; the impulse to say that they have withdrawn from "the real world" comes from this belief that the life of the spirit is less real, less urgent than business, or politics, or engineering, or what have you. Much of our culture, not just religion, has followed this dualistic path. Spirituality has been cut off from earthier pursuits, whether that means issues of the body, of politics, or of agriculture.

For the last several decades, however, a reclaiming of immanence as a proper category of spiritual experience has been growing, as has the recognition that the boundary between these two categories is permeable. Not only are the spiritual and the physical, or the transcendent and the immanent, not incompatible or opposed—they are actually interrelated and complementary. Mainstream Western culture has had to rethink some old assumptions about what is spiritual and what is not, as it embraces embodied Eastern practices such as yoga, feng shui, and forest bathing. Science and medicine have gotten in on the act, too, looking to practices like mindfulness and meditation to address a host of modern ills, from high blood pressure to depression and anxiety.

In terms of my own tradition, mainline Christianity has been slow to embrace this shift. I am happy to say there is a kind of reawakening going on, as we at last begin to remember that this more integrated and holistic understanding of spirituality is not a new perspective but a very old one. Embodied spiritual practices come down to us from our Jewish forebears in faith and are as ancient as lighting candles before prayer or going on pilgrimage. Recent decades have seen a resurgence of interest in Celtic spirituality, in large part because it rejects dualism and centers on the ways in which the natural world can be a window into the realm of the spirit. Many people who have never stepped foot in Ireland or Scotland, for example, know about the existence of "thin places," those locations that (as Eric Weiner wrote in an article for the travel section of the

New York Times) "beguile and inspire, sedate and stir, places where, for a few blissful moments, I loosen my death grip on life, and can breathe again."[1] The intersection of immanence and transcendence, of place and spirit, is gaining traction as a legitimate and meaningful reality.

We might seem to have strayed a fair distance from the start of this chapter and the focus on finding the right spot to plant your begonias, but actually we haven't gone that far afield. I hope that all this talk of immanence and transcendence will help articulate the experience we can find in the garden, which I think is that sweet spot where the horizontal and the vertical axis come together and overlap: the crux, the meeting place of physical and spiritual, earthly and divine, or whatever words make the most sense to you. Let's go back to that idea of "givens." Gardening is a lifelong master class in dealing with reality, with givens. Or, as one of our generation's great chroniclers of the complex relationship between plants and people, Michael Pollan, puts it, "Gardens instruct us in the particularities of place."[2] And it is precisely in paying attention to the particularities that the gardener becomes more attuned to the spiritual resonance of a place.

As much as I love the optimism of the saying "Bloom where you're planted," it glosses over the reality that plants actually care where they're planted, and people should, too. The problem is, most of us don't live as if our location really matters.

Reclaiming Our Space

I was born with no sense of direction. I honestly don't think there's any way I could exaggerate how little spatial awareness I possess. Prior to having a car and a phone with GPS mapping,

I spent so much time lost that I had to schedule for it when I was going somewhere new. It doesn't help that I've tended to be an abstracted person, not paying much attention to my surroundings. Once I was driving my older daughter between our house and the church where I worked, a drive we'd taken dozens, if not hundreds, of times. Stopped at a light, I happened to glance over at the Catholic church that was on the main road I always took for the brief journey, and remarked to my daughter that they must have done a major renovation. Just look at that two-story-high stained-glass Jesus at the front of the church—how magnificent! I went on and on. My daughter shook her head and informed me that two-story stained-glass Jesus was not new but had been there for as long as she could remember. I couldn't believe it, so I called my husband and asked. He had, in fact, grown up going to that church, and he confirmed Annabel's claim. Yep, the two-story stained-glass Jesus had been there for as long as he could remember, too. Somehow, I'd just never noticed it before.

While I might be an extreme case, the truth is that many of us have a pretty limited sense of place. The twentieth century was a time of rapid homogenization of American culture and landscape, with regional differences largely erased by the unending sameness of strip malls, big-box stores, and bland corporate architecture. Nearly every main street has the same shops and restaurants, national chains that offer the same experience, merchandise, and menu whether you're in Ohio, Alabama, or Oregon. Rural landscapes have shifted as well, from a time when small family farms dotted the landscape, with their varied crops and livestock, to this current era of industrial agriculture and its endless acres of high-yield monoculture crops. This context makes it harder than it has ever been to really know the place where you live, to feel its character as a shaping force in your life and personality.

Add to this flattening of our landscape our very American urge to move frequently, always chasing the next educational or career opportunity no matter how far from home it takes us, and you have a culture that is, it would seem, more uprooted and dislocated than any other in human history. This is a major cause of the separation from our food system that is also a hallmark of American culture today, and of so many cultures around the world that have been influenced by ours, characterized not only by fast-food chains but also by massive supermarkets, again offering the same products wherever we live, and the ability to order food online without even having to step out of our front door. It is all terribly convenient, and certainly makes room in our lives for other pursuits. But it creates an enormous gap between our selves and our *givens*, the realities into which we are born and which have limited and shaped all the generations of humanity that came before us, until quite recently. Douglas E. Christie, a scholar who has written extensively on spirituality and ecology, sums it up by saying that in our "highly mobile, technologized, and urban world" many of us feel a sense of "chronic placelessness."[3] "Placelessness" is a word I wish would enter our vocabularies; if we can name and recognize the problem, we can begin to do something about it.

Theologian Norman Wirzba has thought about this condition as deeply as any other writer I know. He writes:

> When people withhold themselves or are prevented from entering deeply into a place, they become disoriented. Disorientation does not simply happen at the location level when,

> for instance, a person does not know which room to be in. Disorientation also goes deeper into a fundamental distortion of *who one should be* and *what one should do*. . . . To fail to know places in detail, and the wisdom that has collectively been learned there, is to lose the possibility of detailed understanding.[4]

Whether we call it disorientation, placelessness, or dislocation, it seems that many of us struggle with this same sense of not quite belonging to the places where we live. Worse yet, many people have no sense of the struggle at all, no realization that there is something fundamental missing from their way of life. After all, you are unlikely to miss something you have never experienced. For too many of us, placelessness has become our lifelong reality.

While not a panacea for all that ails us, gardening does without doubt get us back to the givens, requiring us to grasp at least the basic information about where we live if we want to garden successfully and mindfully, gently repositioning us back in the realities of our location. It starts with something as simple and concrete as knowing the USDA plant hardiness zone where you live, so that when you are choosing which perennials or vegetables to plant you know when to plant them and what their growing season is likely to be where you live. It develops from there, as your time gardening will almost certainly begin to awaken your curiosity about place. You will find yourself noticing other people's plants, perhaps when you're out walking your dog, and wondering if they would thrive as well in your own little patch of ground. You will pay more attention to the weather, if you garden outdoors, and to where your food comes from, especially if you take to growing your own vegetables and begin to replace some of your purchased food with crops you grow and harvest yourself. None of this requires a wholesale abandonment of modern conveniences or a return to a preindustrial way of life. But it does begin the process of grounding our minds and bodies more firmly in the reality of our place, which in the long run is medicine for our souls as well.

Another Given: The March of Time

Before we think a little more about the given of place, I want to point out that gardens help locate us in time as well as place. Gardens are one of those places where time slows down, where it's easy to spend two hours and feel as if no time has gone by at all. This might sound like it is taking us away from reality, but again I'd say that it is more that it is reminding us of a reality deeper than the clock time that ticks away in minutes and seconds. When it comes to time, life today is lived under an exacting specificity that is far from the norm in human history. Gardens push us back into a more natural rhythm, where it matters if it is early morning, midday, or evening, but the division of the hours into smaller and smaller increments feels like a silly irrelevancy. What does thirty minutes mean to a plant? On the other hand, what does noon feel like to a plant, and what might it feel like to us if we are out in a garden in the middle of summer?

At the risk of stating the obvious, a garden takes time. Plants do not grow overnight, nor does a successful harvest occur without significant time spent planting, weeding, watering, and in other ways tending to the garden. Once an investment of time and other resources has been put into creating a church garden, it is likely that congregations will choose to continue the garden from year to year. Those of us who live in climates where active gardening is not a year-round activity nonetheless find that we spend time in non-gardening months thinking about and planning our gardens. We also learn that gardens can shape our sense of time; they cannot be hurried, nor can pressing garden work be put off for a later date or a more convenient time. Plants need what care they need when they need it. Church gardening is not a Sunday-only activity, which is crucial to its formative power. Members have to come back to church during the week to tend the garden, even if they share a schedule and take turns with the garden activities.

A year of gardening is just a year of gardening—it is not quite the same thing as *having* a garden, which is something that reappears spring after spring after spring. With many church or community programs today, spending a "whole year" on something feels like a very long time. I have been told by supposed experts that no adult learners want to take a class that lasts more than four weeks. While I suppose you could learn a lot about gardening in four weeks of classroom time, the amount of gardening you can *do* in four weeks is a different matter altogether. In this way gardening is closer to our most fundamental spiritual practices, like prayer or worship, than to most programs or courses. You need to do it over a long period of time, year in and year out really, for it to sink in and become a part of who you are.

When it comes to church gardens specifically, there is an even longer-scale issue of time at work. While growing vegetables at church may feel new or even trendy, there is a long history of gardens and small-scale agriculture on church property.

This "trend" is therefore more accurately understood as an older model of stewardship of the land or a reclaiming of our tradition. Of course, church gardens do not take us back in time, but they do connect us to our past and, ideally, demonstrate an intentional connection to our future.

This is true of other types of gardens as well. As Stanford professor of French and Italian literature Robert Pogue Harrison writes, "History without gardens would be a wasteland. A garden severed from history would be superfluous."[5] Harrison's book about gardens as cultural artifacts of human care and attention is a testimonial to the accuracy of this assertion. He writes about both secular and religious gardens as they have influenced literature and culture for several centuries. Nor does he confine himself to Europe and America, for he also considers Japanese Zen gardens. Another book of equally rich cultural scope and historical breadth is scholar and priest David Brown's *God and Enchantment of Place*, which has a chapter comparing Christian, Buddhist, and Islamic gardens over the course of several centuries.[6] Gardens as symbols, as literary tropes, and as actual places are profoundly important to nearly every culture across the globe and throughout human history.

A Word about Lawns

One of the things that prompted me to start a garden at my parish in St. Louis was my antipathy toward the lawn. As lawns go, it was a beauty—smooth, green, mostly flat—and there were acres of it. At first, I didn't have a problem with it. The size of the lawn was consistent with those maintained by most residential properties in the area and had perhaps been created with the intention of aligning the appearance of the church property with the rest of the neighborhood. And that was where my misgivings began; I started noticing how many people had trouble finding the church, even when they had the address and were looking for it. Forget about anyone stumbling onto us because they just happened to be walking by. We fit in too well, utterly adapted not to the natural landscape but to the culture of homogeneity that was 1950s midwestern suburbia, the time and place of the church's construction.

Looking back at our discussion of placelessness and the American landscape, a big rolling lawn is almost as emblematic of the issue as a supermarket or fast-food restaurant. Michael Pollan's book *Second Nature* contains a compelling argument about lawns as metaphor and status symbol in the United States. He explores the deeper meaning implied in how people choose to conform (or not) to the suburban ideal of an uninterrupted expanse of green lawn and all the implied embrace of egalitarianism and democracy that goes along with that decision. There can be an unpleasant coerciveness to this kind of cultural conformity; Pollan quotes a nineteenth-century landscape designer who despised fences and hedgerows in suburban front yards, declaring in all seriousness that "it is unchristian . . . to hedge from the sight of others the beauties of nature which it has been our good fortune to create or secure."[7] Pollan concludes that this "deep-seated distrust of individualistic approaches to the landscape" is still alive and quite widespread in American culture today.

Lawns are not just a problem at the metaphorical or cultural level, with their bland sameness that contributes to the flattening of our spaces, the loss of specificity and character. The lawn at my parish was typical in that it was expensive to maintain and detrimental to the environment. We hired a company that used a large ride-on mower to cut the grass, consuming irreplaceable fossil fuels and creating both noise and air pollution. Lawns need a lot of water and are usually maintained with pesticides and chemical fertilizers, which then end up in runoff. Because of the environmental costs of large expanses of lawn, many experts are recommending replacing lawn with shrubs, native grasses, meadows, drought-tolerant ground cover, or whatever is most appropriate in your climate and context. This anti-lawn movement is certainly gaining traction where I live in the American West, where water shortages are spurring people into considering new and creative options for their front and back yards.

My discontent with the church's lawn peaked around the same time that the parish itself was grappling with what to do with a property that had more land than it needed. At a time when many places of worship struggle with large, old buildings that are expensive to maintain and underutilized, we had a building that was the right size but grounds that were too large for our needs. As noted earlier, I knew we had to do something to make it more of an asset for our community. But how? I finally raised it with the parish, explaining that I felt we were sitting on an asset that had the potential to be life-changing for us, but only if we put some concerted effort into discerning a new direction to take. This was the beginning of a fruitful and faithful conversation, one that I believe is happening in more and more communities around the country as an asset-based, community-oriented approach to the properties owned by faith groups becomes more common.

My first idea was to raise goats and create a small social enterprise that would sell goat's milk cheese and other products. I imagined converting three or four acres into a small farm, with chickens and honeybees as well as goats. Remember, I've always been a bit of a dreamer, as well as an animal lover. Not only was the church leadership wary of this idea, but it turned out we would never get the required permits from our city, which did not encourage the raising of livestock, even on properties that had the room for it. Happily, we soon landed on the idea of a garden. It turned out that we had plenty of gardeners in our congregation, and one couple in particular who had dreamed of starting a communal garden for some time. The process took off from there. There were doubters, of course, and a lot of logistical issues to sort out, but a garden that would grow food for those in our community who were facing food insecurity turned out to be something that people could rally around.

And so a big chunk of lawn came out, and in its place grew vegetables, flowers, and fruit—a prolific garden that helped feed dozens of people in its first year, and many, many more in the years that followed. Nobody missed that patch of grass when it was gone. We were too busy tending to our garden beds, working out how to capture rainwater, weighing and delivering produce, and attending myriad other tasks that demonstrated how alive and fruitful that little plot of land had become.

From Wilderness to Garden: A Personal Journey

The English language does not have a word to describe the opposite of the placelessness and dislocation I wrote about earlier, except perhaps the simple word "belonging," which can mean many other things as well. Scholars sometimes speak of a "theology of place," which comes close but is a bit too abstract and academic for what is in fact an embodied, almost visceral experience of awakened awareness and knowing. Poet, essayist, and Kentucky farmer Wendell Berry calls it "ecological intelligence," a phrase I find helpful.[8] Understanding about different types of intelligence and modes of learning has exploded in recent years, and the reality of an ecological intelligence deserves far more attention than it has received. One could persuasively argue that it was among the most essential attributes for humans for most of our history, for without it our ancestors were unlikely to succeed as either hunter-gatherers or farmers. That it must have been so necessary for so long leads me to believe that it cannot have been lost to us entirely in a matter of a hundred years or so. Rather, I imagine it as simply underutilized and flabby, a muscle that needs to be strengthened, mostly forgotten but not in fact gone.

The story of my own evolving levels of ecological intelligence is probably not so different from what many others have experienced, at least in its broad outlines. But since one of the main points of this chapter is to move from generalities to the particulars of place, I will share a bit more detail to illustrate the movement from an intimate knowing of the places where I lived to a loss of that rooted and embodied knowledge and then to my rerooting of myself as a gardener. Perhaps you will find yourself drawn to outline your own life in a similar manner—by how connected you have been at different times to the places in your life. You might want to make some notes about your own geographic autobiography, almost like writing a spiritual autobiography; even if you have moved around less than I have, there will have been times in your life when place has meant more to you and other times when it has meant less.

I have already shared how my early childhood was spent with my feet firmly on the ground—in the dirt, really, as I loved to be barefoot and often had to head straight to the bathtub when I came inside before dinner, my feet stained purple from the olives I had tromped on while playing under the shade of olive trees in our front yard. Those early years of making mud pies and picking smelly wildflowers were lived in a part of northern California that is in between the Bay Area and the Central Valley, a place of foothills that turn golden brown in the summer and miles and miles of orchards that blossom in pink and white profusion in the spring. I did not realize how much that place had embedded itself in my soul until I had been away for many years and, when I came back, found that the smells of certain plants I associated with that region—eucalyptus, jasmine, pine—could make me cry when they caught me unawares.

When I was seven years old we moved to an island in the Pacific, then part of the Trust Territories of Micronesia, and there too I spent hours in imaginative play outside, although now the terrain had changed to tropical rainforest, a jungle so dense and untamed it was a bit like paradise. Everything there was new to me, and heavy with a sense of enchantment. Instead of the dusty green of olive trees and oleander, a yard full of tropical fruit, guava and papaya and banana, greeted me when I stepped out the front door. In northern California it really only rains during the winter months; on our tropical island it rained every day, pouring down in great buckets for at least an hour every afternoon, turning the dirt roads to mud and bringing out toads the size of salad plates from wherever they hid the rest of the day, not to mention a proliferation of enormous African snails that my brother used as target practice with his BB gun. The result of all this rain was that everything that grew there grew thick and fast, from wild ferns to the ever-encroaching mildew against which my mother fought a valiant battle, armed with bleach and her best Dutch cleaning skills. That year I was given a paperback set of the *Chronicles of Narnia* by C. S. Lewis, and I cannot reread those novels without remembering how I would head through the rainforest to a nearby stream, the perfect spot for playing out my own imaginary battles, swinging from heavy vines into the water as I sought to rescue Prince Caspian from some evil that had befallen him and swim him safely back to the *Dawn Treader*, anchored just out of sight in a secluded grotto. My school attendance was sporadic that year, but my love of reading was set alight.

The third defining landscape of my childhood, after the hilly suburbs of Northern California and the rainforests of Micronesia, was perhaps the most formative of all: the long white-sand beaches of Oahu's windward side, where we moved when I was about nine and stayed until after I graduated from high school. It was as idyllic as it sounds. Every day after school I would walk my dog on the beach, which was just a few minutes from our house. I got to know that stretch of sand and water as intimately as any place on earth. There is something about the vastness of the ocean, the endless vista of sea and sky it opens up, that has a profound spiritual dimension to it that affects even the most decidedly materialist people. For me it was a constant source of sublimity and inspiration, the place where I felt most alive and most in touch with God.

To this day the landscapes of my imagination, the ones I know best, are the places where I grew up. Two of them are wilderness landscapes—the rainforest and the ocean. Wilderness is what people are most likely to think of first when they think about having a spiritual connection to place. Ever since Thoreau took off for Walden Pond, we Americans have tended to think that you have to be away from people, far from civilization, if you want to commune with nature in any meaningful way. We flock to the Rocky Mountains, or the Grand Canyon, or the Alaskan outback to have these peak experiences. Gardens might at first seem too homely, too domestic, not grand enough, to be the source of spiritual inspiration.

Steven Charleston, a retired Episcopal bishop and a member of the Choctaw Nation of Oklahoma, has written about the tendency we have to believe that certain special places, "thin places," have more inherent spiritual value than others. He warns against this way of thinking in his book *The Four Vision Quests of Jesus*:

> While I understand that there are many geographical locations that people revere, I do not believe that any of these places are magical portals to transformation. The key to the seeker's quest is not in finding just the right piece of holy real estate on which to stand, but rather in so preparing his or her awareness that any space he or she occupies can become thin through faith.[9]

This was a lesson I had to learn in midlife. Perhaps the places where I lived in my younger days were just too obviously enchanted, if such a thing is possible: I had never had to prepare my awareness to perceive a sense of the sacred.

After bouncing around to different locations on both coasts for college, graduate school, and first jobs for my husband and myself, landing at last in the Midwest for a long stretch was profoundly disorienting. It seemed to me the region had no discernible landmarks or boundaries. How could anyone tell east from west, north from south, when you could get on a freeway and drive for days without hitting a large mountain range, let alone the ocean? It took a few years to settle in and get comfortable. By the time I became rector of that small church in the suburbs, I thought I was as settled as I was going to be. My career was going well, we had nice friends, our children were in good schools—St. Louis had become home.

And yet, in retrospect, I can see that my sense of my new parish as a *place* was highly abstracted. I understood that on accepting a new call I would need to learn about the people in my congregation, and our socio-demographic context. But I knew nothing about the land on which my parish was located. Walking across the parking lot on my way into the office or the church, I could not have told you which way was east, or what part of the property got the most sun during the day. I did not know that the shrubs that bordered the lot were actually an invasive, non-native species of honeysuckle. I did not know if the people who cut our lawn were using fertilizers, or weed killers, or any other kind of poison. Looking back, the list of things I did not know seems endless. My ignorance was so total that for more than two years it did not even occur to me that these were things I ought to know.

It didn't help that I wasn't sure how much I liked the region we were in—again, *as a place*. I liked the people just fine. But I found the St. Louis area awfully drab, even a little ugly. I'm not proud to admit this, as it sounds like the worst kind of snobbery from a "coastal elite." Not finding beauty in the place where I worked was actually a kind of spiritual crisis for me.

I am used to living in places where I can step outside my door and be filled with wonderment and awe. Perhaps it was a form of aesthetic entitlement; at some level I believed that the natural world was there to dazzle me. It had done so since I was a young child, and I had imagined it would always go on doing so. Living in a place where it was often too hot or too cold, too buggy or too humid, a place where there were neither mountains nor oceans nor many wide-open spaces, became a huge challenge. I was like a spoiled child: What is the *point* of going outside if it's not going to *feed* me? What is there to *look at*? How am I supposed to find God *here*, anyway?

There were two things that snapped me out of this unhelpful way of looking at my location. One was a conversation with a wise priest who had also grown up somewhere exotic and beautiful (I believe it was Indonesia, but don't actually remember) and then become a Midwestern transplant, like me. I asked her how she found beauty in the world around her, and she counseled me to start small: look at lichen on a rock, or the texture of bark on a nearby tree. When looked at with enough loving attention, she assured me, every place contains beauty. Again, this reminds me now of the insights of Bishop Charleston: "The shift to the location where the mind can be receptive to an encounter with God begins in the inner reality of the seeker."[10] In other words, if you can't live in a place you love, learn to love the place where you live. Shift your interior landscape.

The other change, of course, was the creation of the garden. It does not take too many days of working in a garden before you really *care* about it. With the wonderful tutelage of more experienced gardeners to guide me, I found myself treating every excursion into the garden like a field trip to an amazing, hands-on children's museum or fantastic laboratory. There was so much to learn. I wanted to know all those givens we've discussed earlier—the type of soil we had, the amount of rain we were likely to get from week to week and month to month, the critters that were most likely to invade our little wonderland. And so much more: why did we plant certain plants where we did, how long would the seeds take to germinate, what was the likelihood of success for tomatillos (something none of us had grown before), how tall would those sunflowers get, when is broccoli ready to be harvested? Every day brought new questions, new problems to solve, and new insights. Knowing that the plants we were growing would become a delicious meal for someone without a regular source of fresh, healthful produce just made the stakes higher and the emotional investment greater.

Very soon, I realized that I loved the garden. I loved the way it looked, the way it smelled, the good things it was achieving. In writing about the love of place, Wendell Berry has said:

> I do not mean any kind of abstract love, which is probably a contradiction in terms, but particular love for particular things, places, creatures, and people, requiring stands and acts, showing its successes or failures in practical or tangible effects. And it implies a responsibility just as particular, not grim or merely dutiful, but rising out of generosity.[11]

That was my experience with the garden exactly. I felt responsible for it, and that responsibility became life-giving, energizing, and central to my sense of vocation. I cared about it and wanted to know everything there was to know about it. It was not, in a sense, so very different from being a mother with a newborn, counting every little finger and toe over and over again, knowing the smell of your baby's head and the particular sound of each gurgle and cry.

During the ordination service in the Episcopal Church, the new priest promises to "love and serve the people among whom I work." While I took that vow very seriously, I was nonetheless under the delusion that love was something that could be separated from place. But location, as we have seen, matters. If you love the little plot of earth where your congregation meets and worships, holds funerals and baptizes babies, eats potlucks and hosts recovery meetings—if you love that place, you are going to find your love for the people strengthened and renewed. Perhaps not everyone needs a garden in order to achieve that kind of love, but for me it was the gateway to a new relationship with my parish, my town, and the earth. I loved the people of my parish better because I loved the land now, too. My love had become less abstract, more generous, and more responsible because it became more grounded in the primary given of place.

Robert Pogue Harrison writes, "There are no states of soul that do not have their proper place in the world; and if there were no places in the world there would be no soul in it either."[12] This was the conversion that happened to me in the garden: I went from having no proper place in the world to acknowledging the garden as my place. Gardens will do that to you—if you let them.

Rogation Days and Holy Neighborliness

The growing popularity of church gardens has led to a renewed interest in rogation days, a practice I heartily endorse as another way to improve our communal sense of connection to place. I'll

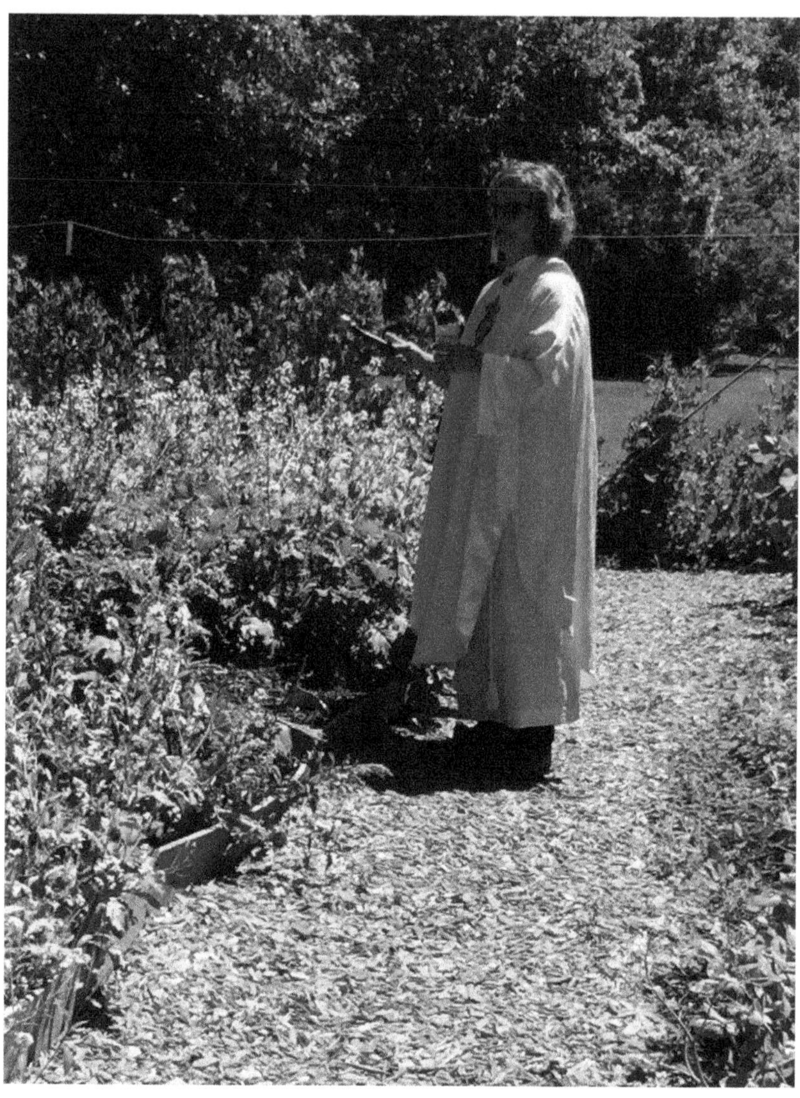

The author blessing Shepherd Farm. Credit: Leslie Scoopmire

explain what they are in a Christian context; I'm certain they could be easily adapted to other traditions.

Imagine, if you will, a small parish church in rural England. It is the year of our Lord thirteen hundred and something or other. The big day has finally arrived. Not Christmas, not Easter, but the start of Rogationtide.

For three days before the Feast of the Ascension (a holy day that occurs forty days after Easter Sunday), everyone who lives within the geographical boundaries of the parish will gather together for a series of processions. They will all march around with banners and crosses and holy water. Bells will be rung and litanies chanted. People will enthusiastically beat the edges of the field with sticks, both to mark out the physical limits of the parish and to beat away any demons or evil spirits that might be lurking in the hedgerows.

This ritual has come to be known either as "beating the bounds" or as "charming the fields." Sometimes young boys get hold of the sticks and take whacks at one another. Sometimes groups from different parishes meet up on the borders and fights break out. Always at the end of it all there will be food and drink provided by parish bigwigs, so that those who are less fortunate can enjoy a bit of ease and pleasure.

Largely forgotten after the Reformation, these rituals were once as vital to the formation of a shared parish identity as anything that occurred during the liturgical year, either inside or outside the church building. They had both religious and social functions, and they remind us that for most of human history religion has been primarily a communal activity, not an individual one.

The great scholar of church history Eamon Duffy contends that what gave these processions their power was that they became occasions of "holy neighborliness" for the community.[13] In other words, they drew people together, reminding them that their identity as Christians depended on being a part of the body of Christ, something much bigger than their individual selves or households. I can only imagine what a remarkable thing it would be if Christians today were known for our "holy neighborliness." This is more than just a matter of being nice, mind you, more than letting the person next door borrow a bag of sugar or a couple of eggs. This is about recognizing our complete interdependence, not only in physical matters but in spiritual ones as well.

And all this came about because the church recognized the importance of people knowing their place, not in the derogatory sense of knowing their place in society but in the literal sense of knowing where they belonged on the land, what the actual boundaries were between their parish and the next. I am glad that some churches are recovering this tradition; if it ever really catches on, it could be the beginning of a much deeper understanding of place and how it shapes us, individually and collectively. This move toward knowing our places of worship *as places* can help us become more rooted in the world and make any place where we work, live, or play into "holy real estate."

Discussion Questions

1. What physical things in life give you a sense of place?
2. What spiritual things give you a sense of place?
3. How has the landscape of your life changed? How have you changed in how you navigate it?
4. How can a garden alter the landscape of our lives together?

CHAPTER THREE

GROUNDING OURSELVES IN SOIL

Credit: iStock.com/CasarsaGuru

Don't treat your soil like dirt. That might be the most basic lesson that every gardener needs to learn—at least every gardener who wants to work in harmony with the earth and not rely on chemical interventions.

"Dirt" is a four-letter word. There are a lot of four-letter words I rather like, if I'm being real, and "dirt" is one of them. It has an honesty and a punch to it. Dirt is nothing to be ashamed of—all our houses and cars and bodies build up a certain level of dirt, and it can be invigorating to scrub them down and wash them clean. But dirt is not the same thing as soil.

Soil is the basic building block of a garden, and one of the basic building blocks of life on this planet. Not as basic as carbon or oxygen, but related to them in important ways. A famous aphorism sums up how integral soil is: "Despite all our achievements we owe our existence to a six-inch layer of topsoil and the fact that it rains."[1] It's hard for most of us living in the industrialized West to believe this at our core. On a day-to-day basis, the weather is either convenient or inconvenient—good weather is a pleasure, bad weather is a pain in the neck—but it doesn't fundamentally affect whether we have enough to eat. There is always the supermarket, the fast-food outlet, the farmers' market, or even an online outfit that will deliver food to our dinner plates in no time at all and with minimal effort or forethought required of us.

Similarly, if you are not a farmer or gardener, you might never have considered the existence of topsoil, let alone how important it is to your survival. Even if you are a gardener, our society encourages you to find all your solutions through consumption. When you're planting vegetables or rosebushes or what have you, you might go to a big-box store, one of thousands of identical places in every corner of the country, and buy bags of soil and haul them home. You might have no idea where the soil comes from, how far it has traveled in its thick plastic covering, or what its carbon footprint is. You will likely be encouraged to buy fertilizers, too. If you're feeling virtuous and have the extra cash, you will buy something labeled organic. That's about as much as many of us know about the stuff we put our seeds or seedlings into, blindly trusting that it will be good enough to create the growth we desire.

Most of the time, it is good enough. This transactional model has its limits, though. Soil procured in this way is as impersonal as a TV dinner and just about as convenient (if possibly more nutritious). It is hard to think of yourself as having a relationship with this soil. It feels more like an anonymous part of our consumer-based culture, not something alive and specific, something with a history and particular gifts and attributes.

In fact, though, soil has all those qualities: life, specificity, history, place, and rich gifts to offer. For nonscientists like myself, the basic distinction between dirt and soil is that soil is alive. Soil provides a foundation for growth that is much more than a simple, inert place to stick a plant, like a layer of floral foam that just happens to be underfoot. It is a dense ecosystem all its own.

Consider this: a mere handful of soil has more living organisms than there are people on the planet. Some of these living organisms you can see for yourself with minimal effort. Go out to any healthy garden bed and root around for a bit in the soil. You shouldn't have to dig for long before you find earthworms. You will likely find other creepy-crawly things in there, too—and by and large, this is a good thing. There are pests in gardens, too, of course, but not every uninvited critter is a problem.[2] Healthy soil will have both visible and microscopic creatures of various kinds, including protozoa, nematodes, and arthropods, not to mention bacteria and fungi. Taken together, these make up a specific soil food web.[3]

Your investigation of soil might also turn up some things that don't appear to be alive, but are—tendrils and threadlike filaments extending from the roots of your plants, little things that to an untrained eye might look like the roots themselves but are actually part of a complex system known as mycorrhizae. This word looks like quite a mouthful at first, but it breaks down into two Greek roots (forgive the pun): *myco*, having to do with fungus, and *rhiza*, meaning root. Mycorrhizal associations are simply the relationships between roots and certain fungi, which are symbiotic, or mutually beneficial, and, in some cases, necessary for the plant to exist at all.[4]

Once a subject known only to botanists, mycorrhizae are having a bit of a moment in the popular imagination. Back in 1997, the journal *Nature* published an article by a young forest ecologist named Suzanne Simard, who was researching a "cryptic underground fungal network" in a forest that was "connecting all the trees in a constellation of tree hubs and fungal links."[5] *Nature* called this network "the wood-wide web," and the clever name helped popularize Simard's findings, sometimes in a way that has led to less-than-rigorous leaps of logic by nonspecialists like myself. Nonetheless, there are genuinely stunning insights in Simard's work, and she has done much to make it available to the general public, in lectures, interviews, and now a book that is part memoir and part popular science tome, *Finding the Mother Tree.*

Mycorrhizal associations not only help feed an individual plant but also connect plants to one another, creating below-ground networks of communication and resource sharing. Maybe you've heard of research that suggests that plants thrive when we talk to them. Well, now there is research showing that plants need to "talk" to each other—research that is far more convincing than the average science fair project looking at what happens when you strike up a conversation with your lima bean plants. A healthy garden, like a healthy forest, will be a place where these complex underground networks are robust and thriving.

The bottom line is that most of the life in your garden is belowground, in the soil, and most of the life in your soil is invisible to the human eye, being made up of bacteria and fungi that you can only see with a microscope. There's a lot going on in the soil of any healthy garden bed that is necessary for successful plant growth, but because it happens out of sight it mostly goes unnoticed—until something goes wrong and the gardener has to try to figure out how to fix it. If you don't want to take a course in biology to understand exactly what is going on at this microscopic level, fear not. The basics of soil science are not hard to master through a gardening class or even with a little judicious web searching. But don't be surprised if, once you get started learning about this topic, you end up slightly obsessed with it.

Like so much else in the natural world, the more you learn about soil, the more you will realize you don't know. This can be daunting, or it can be exciting. Scientists themselves are just beginning to recognize how complex soil is. Michael Pollan put his own epiphany about the living nature of soil this way:

> Much more than an inert mechanism for conducting water and chemicals to the crop's roots, it actually contributed nutrients of its own making to the plants. The biology, chemistry, and physics of this process, which goes by the name "fertility," is not at all well understood—soil truly is a wilderness—yet this ignorance doesn't prevent organic farmers and gardeners from nurturing it.[6]

Soil is a wilderness: a place of adventure and mystery that is awaiting exploration. It is also the home of one of the most essential networks of interspecies relationships yet discovered on our planet, the mycorrhizal associations that thrive under the surface of forests and gardens alike. In all these ways and more, soil is a great teacher.

Humus and Humility

Once we understand what soil is—a complex, living ecosystem—the spiritual lessons that it holds are limitless. Theologically, the saying "don't treat your soil like dirt" is a recognition that even soil is a gift from God, a miracle. Without it, we would not be alive—not a single one of us. Whenever I hear people talking about soil this way, with awe and wonder, with gratitude and respect, I feel like I'm in the presence of the holy. People who understand, even intuitively, how miraculous soil is are people I feel like I can trust. If they don't take soil for granted, they aren't likely to take for granted the more obvious members of the web of life—like you and me.

So, it seems that gratitude might be the first spiritual lesson and practice we can draw from our garden's soil. The notion that such a humble substance, something so easily overlooked and underappreciated, is full of mystery and complexity ought to leave us in awe of nature's ways, and in my experience awe and wonder almost always lead to gratitude. We might find ourselves looking twice at the vegetables on our dinner plate—this carrot, this potato, grew in soil. How cool is that? If you grew those vegetables yourself, the connection will come more easily; after all, you have to wash that soil off the carrot's skin before peeling and eating or cooking it. If you're not yet growing your own vegetables, buying them in as natural and unprocessed a state as possible might help. Yes, sometimes I still buy bags of carrots that are already cleaned, peeled, and cut down to size. But when I go to a farmers' market and instead buy a bunch of carrots with the greens still attached, the few extra minutes it takes to prepare them almost always become an opportunity for thinking about the soil and the farmer who made these carrots possible. How could I *not* feel grateful? Some patch of earth grew these carrots. Some farmer tended them and pulled them from the ground at just the right moment. How lucky I am that they did that work for me, so that I can have something to eat. This leads me back to the realization that it is not just this particular meal and this particular carrot—rather, all food, all meals, start in the soil, in one way or another. I'm a vegetarian, but if you eat meat, that meat comes from animals that had to eat plants that needed soil for their growth. There is no escaping the necessity for soil, and thus no end to our opportunities for gratitude.

If all this sounds a bit too "out there," let's return to the Bible for a moment to see a different way that we might consider the wonder of soil. In Chapter One we looked at the second creation story in Genesis. You'll remember that in this creation myth, God created man (yes, specifically the first male specimen of humanity) from dirt: "In the day that the Lord God made the earth and the heavens . . . the Lord God formed man from the dust of the ground, and breathed into his nostrils the breath of life; and the man became a living being." Given what we now know about soil, we might want to rethink the dynamic involved in this form of creation. (Again, a quick reminder that I am not suggesting we take this myth literally, but rather that we see it as a story with rich potential to teach us something about God, about ourselves, and about the natural world.) When God breathed life into humanity, the material God used for that first human being was not really dirt or dust, as in something dry, lifeless, and inorganic. It was humus—good dirt, rich, fertile soil, the foundation of life on earth. God did not take something inert and add life. God took something teeming with potential, full of creative energy, and added a spark of the divine.

Thinking of ourselves as "dust" is humbling, which is not entirely a bad thing. Thinking of ourselves as formed from soil is more evocative, while still in keeping with the spirit of the passage from Genesis. Remembering first that soil is alive, a veritable web of networks of living organisms, we might find ourselves realizing with astonishment that you could describe human beings in much the same way. We too are host to an almost incalculable number of microorganisms, some small

Credit: iStock.com/valentinrussanov

number of which are harmful or neutral to our health, but many of which make our existence possible. The gut microbiome, for instance, can be a key indicator of health. Made up of scores of bacteria and other microbes that live in our intestinal tract, the gut microbiome affects not just digestion but also mood and cognitive function. It's not only the gut, though—microbes are all over our bodies, causing some scientists and philosophers to think of human beings as more of a host to a community of these organisms than as discrete, individual bodies all our own.

The lesson in this myth then becomes the same as the lesson that soil itself will teach us—if we are willing to learn. All life on earth is interconnected and interdependent. It is a web, a network, an ecosystem; in a word, it is community. Soil is teeming with life, a rich variety of organisms and microorganisms that both compete and cooperate and, through their complex interactions, form something greater than the sum of the soil's parts. The same can be said aboveground.

The humility we might feel at being made up of soil—or of a bunch of bacteria and other microbes—is tempered by the insight that soil itself is wondrous and miraculous. Soil is a web of life connected to other webs of life, all part of a larger whole, as are we. In the garden, we get an up close and personal view of how these various webs intersect. In the garden, we see how community works.

Feet on the Ground

Even with all this in mind, we have barely touched on how miraculous soil really is. If people were only made up of dirt, we would still be something infinitely beautiful and important. And the truth is, we know we are so much more than just our physical presence, as rich and creative and wondrous as that is.

There is a slightly quirky practice I'd like to suggest as part of your foray into contemplative gardening: garden barefoot. Not all the time, of course, and not if you don't know the terrain pretty well. But being barefoot in the garden, or in your backyard, or on a hiking path, even for short periods of time, can bring about a physical sense of connection to the earth, the ground under our feet, that is hard to come by any other way.

If gardening barefoot is too much of a stretch, then by all means at least try gardening without gloves once or twice and see how you like it. There are times when gardeners absolutely need the protection of gloves, so use common sense. But in our ultraclean, hypoallergenic, fully sanitized world, literally putting your hands in dirt can be such a treat. At a practical level, some garden tasks actually benefit from the extra dexterity that being bare-handed brings; when I am transplanting little seedlings with fragile roots into the ground, I rarely use gloves, because it is just so much easier to be sensitive to the kind of handling the young plants need without them.

Once you've spent some time in the garden barefoot or bare-handed, you could extend the ritual aspect of this practice by giving thanks for the soil before you wash it off. You might also find yourself giving thanks for the water, another miraculous element of life. It's been my experience that when I regularly, intentionally express gratitude for simple, everyday things like dirt and water, I become much more likely to spontaneously feel grateful throughout my day. Not only that, but this practice might well lead us to want to look for beauty and wonder in other humble things, not to mention people and places that we might otherwise overlook.

Gardens as Community

The lesson about interconnectedness and community that we learn first from the soil extends upward into the aboveground parts of the garden as well. Plants are living beings. They may not have consciousness in the way we usually understand it, but they do form relationships with other plants. Certain kinds of plants don't get on well, like prickly in-laws or squabbling siblings, and should not be grown too close to each other, as they will end up in an unhealthy competition for resources.

At the same time, one of the worst things for most plants is to be grown in isolation or only with their own kind. We might love the look of fields and fields of tulips, for instance, or feel a swell of sentiment when we think of "amber waves of grain" and endless acres of cornfields in the great farmlands that form the heart of America. But we indulge in this aesthetic delight at a cost. Monoculture is an increasingly controversial practice, especially in the eyes of people who are concerned with climate change and care for creation.

Celebrated author and botanist Robin Wall Kimmerer summarizes one of the weaknesses of the monoculture approach, which is its vulnerability to pests:

> Polycultures—fields with many species of plants—are less susceptible to pest outbreaks than monocultures. The diversity of plant forms provides habitats for a wide array of insects. Some, like corn worms and bean beetles and squash borers, are there with the intent of feeding on the crop. But the diversity of plants also creates habitat for insects who eat the crop eaters. Predatory beetles and parasitic wasps coexist with the garden and keep the crop eaters under control. More than people are fed by this garden [i.e., a garden grown as a polyculture] but there is enough to go around.[7]

I love the generosity of that description of a garden that incorporates diversity: there is enough to go around. What if we thought this way about human communities? Diversity adds resilience and helps us to realize that there really is enough to go around. I once saw this wonderfully illustrated in a garden grown on the grounds of Zaytuna College, a school rooted in the Islamic scholarly tradition. The administrator giving a tour of the permaculture garden on the school's grounds noted that because they don't use chemical pesticides, some of the fruits and vegetables never get harvested; instead, they are eaten by birds, bugs, or other hungry creatures. The gardeners on the tour groaned; we all know what it's like to find a strawberry or a tomato that looks perfect on one side but has a big bite or a deep hole marring the other, making it less than ideal for harvesting. He chuckled when he noted that the Muslim faith places a high value on feeding those in need and sharing resources; he saw the garden as helping to fulfill that core value by sharing its bounty with its nonhuman neighbors. It is hard for me to remember this perspective when I'm tossing a half-eaten peach into the compost pile because the birds got to it before me, but I do try.

Most of us reading this book will never have to be responsible for pest control on the scale of, say, a thousand acres of soybeans. But even little backyard gardens can be models of diversity. Plants like variety. Left to their own devices, such as in fields or hedgerows, they will seem almost to seek out other plants that they want to live near and interact with. When gardeners learn the combinations of plants that form beneficial relationships when grown together, that is known as companion planting. You can find lists of vegetables illustrating who likes to be paired with whom, and who prefers to keep their distance from certain other plants.

For instance, marigolds are a good companion plant for many common garden vegetables, especially those that, like them, are most comfortable in warm, sunny weather. I often plant marigolds around the same bed where I am growing tomatoes. Both positively scream "summer" to me, although in Northern California, where I live, both will continue producing well into the fall. They are colorful, cheerful plants that don't require much extra attention to thrive. I also love the smell of both plants, although some people find one or the other repellent—and apparently so do some bugs. Marigolds are one of many common plants you can grow as a safe, nontoxic deterrent against certain garden pests like aphids and flea beetles. As more than one website warns, hard science doesn't always confirm the usefulness of such pairings, so you should consider this an opportunity for learning through trial and error.

Our interest here, however, is not in the precise relationships you might choose to cultivate in your garden but in the larger point that relationships exist in the garden at all. And they do. Both in the soil and aboveground, complex interactions between roots and fungi, vegetables and flowers, plants and insects, are all creating a series of associations that can best be understood as a community. Suzanne Simard puts it well: "Plants are attuned to one another's strengths and weaknesses, elegantly giving and taking to attain exquisite balance. A balance that can also be achieved in the simple beauty of a garden." She goes on to note the ways in which the balance achieved in a healthy community of plants mirrors the balance we seek in our own communities: "We can find this in ourselves, in what we do alone, but also in what we enact together. Our own roots and systems interlace and tangle, grow into and away from one another and back again in a million subtle moments."[8] This has certainly been my own experience with my family and friends; there are seasons of intense intimacy and other seasons when there is a bit more emotional distance between myself and a loved one. Drawing closer to one person might, for a time, seem to weaken my connection to someone else. But overall, strong connections lead not only to good emotional health but also to additional strong connections. Because these connections are mutual—I am receiving as well as giving—they do not work like a zero-sum game.

Parenting can be a revelation on this front. Like so many parents before me, I loved my first child with such intensity that I wondered if I could ever love another child enough; was it even a good idea to try having another? And then her little sister was born, and my attachment and devotion were just as strong with her as they had been with my firstborn. Maternal love was not a finite resource; multiple strands of connection were just as hardy and robust as one strand had been. As Robin Wall Kimmerer says, there is enough to go around.

Community and the Three Sisters Garden

At my current parish, when we were looking for a theme for our Care for God's Creation team, we came up with the tagline "Healthy Soil, Healthy Plants, Healthy Communities." The through line was clear to us, although it has taken some explaining to a wider audience. If I had to come up with an elevator pitch, a thirty-second speech to explain why someone should care about our initiative, I might say something like this: "Communities are only as healthy as their individual members, and eating a local and mostly plant-based diet is good for everyone. In order for the plants we eat to be healthy, our soil has to be healthy. Plus, getting out in a garden to grow food and improve soil is a healthy activity that builds community." Okay, so that might be longer than thirty seconds, but you get the idea.

One of the best lessons about how community is grown aboveground as well as belowground in a garden comes from the example of Three Sisters gardens. The Three Sisters are corn, squash, and beans, and growing them together, in close proximity and in a specific order, has long been practiced in many indigenous communities in North America. There are many opinions about the "right" way to structure a Three Sisters garden, but the general idea is simple to the point of ingenuity. Corn is planted in the center of a mound of soil, with one or more bean seeds planted around each corn stalk, close enough so that the corn can form the "pole" or support around which the beans will grow. Squash completes the trio. There is an almost perfect symbiosis among these three plants.

In return for the structural support given them by the corn and the protective cover given by the squash, the beans give the soil a boost of nitrogen, that essential nutrient required for plant growth that must be "fixed" in the soil in order to be accessed. Many gardeners supplement soil with chemical fertilizers in order to add more usable nitrogen, but beans will do that work for you. And wouldn't you know that it does this task through its mycorrhizal associations, those interweavings of roots and fungi we learned about earlier.

The wandering, broad-leafed squash, meanwhile, keeps the soil moist and reduces the need for watering in the heat of the summer, when the other two plants are at the peak of their productivity. The shape of the leaves and their texture also help deter other plants and some insects from making a home—or a meal—where the corn and beans are growing. So aboveground and within the soil the Three Sisters are helping each other thrive, each by doing what comes naturally.

My introduction to Three Sisters gardens came from a book. *Braiding Sweetgrass: Indigenous Wisdom, Scientific Knowledge, and the Teachings of Plants* is a book that is creating a quiet, slow-burning revolution among readers, gardeners, and people who simply care about the earth and how we are treating it. The author, Robin Wall Kimmerer, is a member of the Potawatomi Nation, as well as a crafter of exquisite prose. Her chapter on the Three Sisters garden must be read in full, savored for its wisdom and beauty, and reread on a regular basis—it is without doubt one of the best sermons I have ever heard, teaching with poetry and precision about the sacred duty we all have to use the gifts we have been given, both in order to be the best versions of ourselves we can be and also in order to offer our strength and our giftedness to the communities of which we are a part. I cannot do justice to the richness and sheer persuasive power of her work here, so I will just have to share a bit of the text. She writes:

> Of all the wise teachers who have come into my life, none are more eloquent than these, who wordlessly in leaf and vine embody the knowledge of relationship. Alone, a bean is just a vine, squash an oversize leaf. Only when standing together with corn does a whole emerge which transcends the individual. The gifts of each are more fully expressed when they are nurtured together than alone. In ripe ears and swelling fruit, they counsel us that all gifts are multiplied in relationship. This is how the world keeps going.[9]

Suzanne Simard also writes about her own experiences of growing a Three Sisters garden, something she did while she was mourning the death of a loved one. It appealed to her in part because it seemed congruent with what she was learning about diversity and community in a forest to eschew the usual straight rows of vegetables and try a type of garden designed around supporting the mutually beneficial relationships between plants. She reports that after the corn, beans, and squash were all well established, she pulled up a bean (a small sacrifice for the sake of satisfying her scientific curiosity, I suppose) and "saw tiny white nodules along its length, housing nitrogen-fixing bacteria." She goes on:

> I imagined how the mycorrhizal network played a part in this dance, my garden's network shuttling nitrogen from the nitrogen-fixing beans to the corn and squash. And the tall, sunny corn transmitting carbon to the beans and squash it was shading. And the squash sending the water it had saved to the thirsty corn and beans. My garden thrived.[10]

After all these poetic descriptions of Three Sisters gardens, I feel I must throw in a fair warning: even the most earnest and well-intentioned efforts at companion plantings are not magic. I have had some spectacular failures with Three Sisters gardens, largely because I ignored some basic prerequisites for successful growth. In one case I planted the corn far too late, so it never had a chance to achieve maturity before the weather turned cold, and another time I chose a spot that was simply too shady, while also neglecting to water the new plants sufficiently. Even the hardiest and most companionable members of a garden community can't overcome those odds. Ignoring the basics is never a good idea in gardening, no matter how much optimism and good vibes we sprinkle on top like fairy dust. This might be a lesson, too, especially for those of us prone to wishful thinking and joyful impulsivity. Gardens are resilient, but they don't defy common sense or the laws of biology.

Interestingly, I learned that the Northern California area where I live was not cultivated in this way by its original human inhabitants. In speaking with a culture bearer for the Patwin Wintun people, I began to understand that in this region foraging for nuts and seeds and growing certain crops through scattering seeds was the norm for centuries. That is not to say that corn, squash, and beans can't or don't grow well here, but only to remind myself to be cautious about sweeping generalizations about people, plants, and cultures. Gardening reminds us that "one size fits all" is rarely a true statement, and even small differences in climate, geography, and history matter. I haven't given up on a successful Three Sisters garden, but when next I attempt it I will do so more humbly and with more attention to the realities of context, not assuming that it is somehow foreordained to work out just because the idea of it is so compelling.

Cabbage Worms and Community

Soil is simultaneously alive and the host site for a community of other living beings. In this way and more, people and soil have a lot in common.

Gardening with an eye toward soil health creates community aboveground, too. The gardening practices that make healthy soil possible—reducing tilling, eliminating pesticides, going organic—do require a bit more work than what we sometimes call "conventional" gardening. For example, the need for weeding can be reduced with the right kind of mulch and companion plants, but some manual labor will be involved, probably more than when people spray weed killer and the like. However, adding artificial and potentially poisonous substances to a garden starts to feel odd and incongruous as one begins to settle into the idea of a garden as a place for spiritual practice and contemplation. The fewer the barriers that stand between the soil and the gardener, the more the possibility for a deep connection is being cultivated.

Healthy gardens develop community among plants, as described earlier in the section on companion planting, but also among other creatures. One of the effects of current unhealthy practices in gardens and farms is a loss of biodiversity, meaning that the variety of those other creatures may be reduced, sometimes to levels that endanger plant life and thus our food sources. Climate change and habitat destruction, such as occurs with mining, fracking, urban sprawl, and so on, are also contributing to this problem. When scientists talk about biodiversity, the rest of us probably think "endangered species" and imagine that they are talking about animals and plants that the majority of us will never encounter in the wild. But gardening has taught me that biodiversity is an important issue closer to home, too.

When our gardens begin to imitate the wild profusion of life that nature has to offer, they become something much more than the sum of their parts. The rich belowground diversity of organisms can be mirrored aboveground. A thriving garden with a diverse array of plants draws in pollinators, like bees to nectar (literally). You can choose plants that attract specific creatures you want to see in your garden, such as hummingbirds or monarch butterflies, or you can allow the allure of blossoms and fragrance to do their work naturally and beckon whatever pollinators are native to your area. Many gardeners find that their interest in beneficial insects expands to the point where they are putting out bee homes and even becoming full-fledged beekeepers. This is all part of seeing the garden as a community, an exemplar of interconnection and mutuality in relationships among and between species.

Of course, not all biodiversity is created equal. My first year of gardening at Shepherd Farm, I found myself delighted by daily visits from some elegant white butterflies. Their delicate beauty brought me a sense of something ethereal and fairylike amid the young seedlings pushing up through the earth. I also felt a little surge of self-righteous pleasure: "Our organic practices are yielding an increase in biodiversity!" I silently crowed. After all, I'd never seen those butterflies around the church grounds before.

A month or two later, I was in my office enjoying the sounds of children playing outside. For the first time ever, we were holding our Vacation Bible School in the garden, teaching Bible stories about creation alongside basic botany lessons and gardening skills. The kids were eating it up—sometimes literally, as we incorporated as much of our garden produce in snack time as we possibly could. Suddenly an adult leader rushed into my office, saying there was something going on outside I had to see.

I arrived in the garden to see kids and adults bent over various beds full of young brassicas. There was some squealing from the younger set, accompanied by occasional groans, mostly from the grown-ups. As I got closer, a young boy held up his hand, proudly showing me his treasure: a small, bright green caterpillar, with spiky white hairs poking up along the length of its extremely plump body. I congratulated the boy on his find, to which he replied that we had loads of the things in the garden now. I looked to our VBS leader for confirmation. "Yes," she said, nodding gravely. "It's an infestation—cabbage worms."

For the rest of the morning, it was all hands on deck as we plucked each one of the critters off its chosen vegetation and tossed it into a bucket of soapy water so we could dispose of them as humanely as possible. (True confession: some people smooshed them underfoot, something I could not bring myself to do.) Only while we were working on this gruesome task did the truth hit me: these "worms" were the caterpillar stage of the "pretty white butterflies" I'd seen all over the garden earlier in the season. The butterflies were actually cabbage moths, so called because they lay their eggs on cabbages and other cruciferous vegetables. The dainty little things were leaving unwanted presents during their visits; they were depositing eggs, which had turned into these voracious leaf-eating machines.

So much for the beauty of biodiversity.

Over time, thankfully, we learned ways to fight back against cabbage worm infestations, such as covering their favorite plants with a swath of light fabric, known as row covers, that prevented the moths from landing on them and laying their eggs. We also tried planting more flowers that would attract predators, such as ladybugs and praying mantises, that would make a meal out of the invading worms. Another pest-control method we discovered was adding chickens to our community. A small coop with two lovely hens was all it took, as they happily ate all kinds of bugs, scratched up the soil to keep it aerated, and generously deposited rich organic fertilizer.

While we never had a pest-free garden during my years there, we certainly never again had an infestation like that first one, either. I learned to see it all as part of the cycle of life. I also sternly reminded myself that just because something is pretty doesn't mean it is friendly, nor vice versa; creatures like praying mantises and spiders that give some people the creeps are actually helpful additions to the garden ecosystem, much more friend than foe.

You'll notice that one of the key players in this whole life-and-death cabbage worm drama was the people involved. Human community can also be built in a garden—from the ground up, as I like to say. As I mentioned earlier, some organic methods mean more work; imagine the ease of a one-and-done application of pesticides simply sprayed over our broccoli and brussels sprouts versus the laborious job of picking off hundreds of little, well-camouflaged worm bodies by hand. But it is precisely that kind of work that creates community. Many of the children attending our VBS had more fun that morning than on any other day of the program. We had stories to tell for the rest of the week, stories that were resurrected at the next year's Vacation Bible School and retold with macabre glee. Bragging rights developed around whose worm-picking prowess had proved most effective, and the supposed number of bodies collected grew with each retelling. Volunteers had spent countless hours creating a meaningful, well-researched, age-appropriate curriculum for the camp, and in the end it was nature itself, in all its messy glory, that provided the most memorable lesson.

And this kind of community-building was demonstrated over and over again in the church's garden, not just when the children were present. This should come as no surprise. Psychotherapist Sue Stuart-Smith has researched a number of therapeutic garden programs and written about the results in *The Well-Gardened Mind: The Restorative Power of Nature*. In a conclusion that I find completely congruent with my own experience, she writes, "Cultivating the earth is empowering, and sharing its fruits promotes trust and cooperation more effectively than anything else. We all need to feel a sense of potency and to give and receive nurture. These dual aspects of human nature are brought together through the alchemy of gardening."[11] Trust and cooperation are absolutely critical to a healthy community, and they grow easily in a garden.

A community garden of any significant size requires a team of gardeners, and while it is possible for team members to work in the garden individually, the effort must be coordinated or it can become counterproductive and even harmful. At Shepherd Farm we found that regular communication between gardeners was an essential ingredient of our practice; it was the only way to avoid wasting water, seeds, time, and energy. In our case, we kept a logbook in a waterproof case in the garden and asked people to sign in and keep track of what they did in the garden at each visit.

Some of our gardeners preferred solitary time in the garden, but even when alone they were working as part of a team for all practical purposes. For instance, no one person or subgroup took responsibility for one type of plant or one plot; to the best of our abilities, we were all responsible for the whole garden. At the end of the harvest nobody could really say "*I* grew those turnips" or "*I* made those tomatoes possible"—rather, it was a group effort throughout. It turned out that many people only wanted to help in the garden when they knew there would be others there gardening as well. In part that was a way of learning the practice, much the same way as one might learn to pray by joining a prayer group or even by showing up for worship regularly. In part, too, the fellowship of shared work held its own appeal. The garden became a place of storytelling and getting to know one another. We shared hopes and fears along with our sunscreen and hand tools.

All the skills necessary to garden on a large scale are rarely found in one person, so part of the process of managing a communal garden involves identifying the right people who possess the various necessary skills. There is another kind of biodiversity at work here, as different personalities and skill sets all came together in the same place and for a common purpose. As Shepherd Farm was getting started, for example, some parishioners were adamant that they were not going to bend down and pull weeds, especially not on hot, sunny days, but they turned out to be happy to sit at a picnic table in the shade and weigh the produce as it was harvested. One person only helped on the day we built the fence; that was enough to make him a valued member of the garden community. The community of gardeners we created became something of an ecosystem itself, with one person's skill or knowledge filling in the gaps when another person's fell short. We needed each other; the job was simply too big for it to be left to one or two volunteers.

It turns out that being needed is an underrated element of creating community. In his book *Cultivating Reality: How the Soil Might Save Us*, Episcopal priest and author Ragan Sutterfield writes about the importance of dependence, calling it "a gift without which we wouldn't be human."[12] Gardening and community building both bear out the truth of this insight. We humans need soil, we need what grows in the soil, and we need each other. Recognizing that you need others and in turn are needed by them can be a rich spiritual grace, a source of both gratitude and humility; it is also at the heart of what makes a true community tick.

One of my favorite stories about how the community grew around Shepherd Farm started with what seemed like a potential source of conflict. One of the parishioners was not thrilled by the garden as a project, thinking it would be impossible for our small congregation to maintain. She was an accomplished gardener herself but repeatedly told me that she was too old and too busy to participate in the new endeavor. I assured her that we would not put any pressure on her to take part. A few months in, she stopped me after church to say that something had happened while she was saying her prayers: God had put it on her heart that she should pray for the success of the garden. Episcopalians tend to be pretty reticent in talking about our faith, so this was a big moment for me as a priest, having someone offer such a vulnerable and unprompted testimony about an experience of God in prayer. I told her that would mean the world to me, and that maybe praying for the garden was actually the very best way for her to participate. The following growing season, she ended up out in the garden and soon became one of our most loyal volunteers. Her expertise and hard work were invaluable, and I felt almost as if the garden itself had convinced her to become more involved. It was a bit of a miracle, to be honest.

Wisdom and virtue can be cultivated in a garden community as well as produce can. At Shepherd Farm we focused on thrift and economy, for example, in our use of water: we had children bring in used plastic one-gallon milk jugs when their families were finished with them and taught them how to turn the jugs into a drip irrigation system for our tomato plants. We had spent some grant money we received on purchasing two large rainwater collection drums, so the water used by the homemade drip system was coming to us free of charge, rather than from city water that was added to our bill. It took someone in the community with some engineering know-how to solve a problem this whole setup revealed. Our rainwater barrels were next to the parish hall, whose flat roof and gutters were perfect for collecting water when it rained. But the garden was located uphill from the building, so we spent a lot of our energy filling water jugs from the barrels and then walking up to the garden with them before we could begin watering or refilling the drip system. It was good exercise, admittedly, but it was wearing out the volunteers. The solution turned out to be both simple and ingenious: we built a cistern at the top of the hill, then purchased a solar-powered pump that moved the water from the rain barrels up to the cistern. Gravity did the rest of the work, easily draining the cistern's water into hoses whenever we turned the spigot. (Only much later did it occur to me that this system was not unlike how water travels up the stem of a plant.) Such practical wisdom and resourcefulness were passed along to all who gardened there, giving us all an occasion to think about our own water use at home, as well as how effectively we were repurposing rather than buying new items. The community was strengthened through every one of these exchanges of ideas and expertise.

If you are thinking this is all very nice for those who have a community garden or church garden where they can work and belong, but it doesn't really apply to you, the individual gardener, I hope you will think again. It has been my experience that gardeners are among the most generous and convivial of people, unstinting in their willingness to teach others and share knowledge. There are numerous ways to become part of a community of gardeners, whatever your skill level. You can take a class, online or in person, or even work on becoming certified as a Master Gardener. You can follow garden-oriented social media accounts; the larger ones will have opportunities for webinars and other interactive events. Show up at local plant sales and see if anyone there is looking for volunteers, and do the same if you have a botanical garden or arboretum nearby.

If you're gardening on your own, you will still find that there are endless books, blogs, and programs that will help you get through any difficulty. What became clear to me as I spent more time with gardeners was that nearly all of them consider themselves beginners, or at least lifelong learners. There is a humility to most gardeners that is refreshing, especially in a world of instant experts fueled by YouTube tutorials and Wikipedia searches. (To be clear, both YouTube and Wikipedia can be excellent sources of gardening advice in a pinch. It's just that there's nothing like talking to another gardener to really learn the ropes.) Don't be shy. I've even known people to strike up deep friendships that start with a compliment to a neighbor about their beautiful hydrangea bushes. Gardeners find each other.

And if you are a more experienced gardener, I would urge you to find ways to be part of a gardening community; I can assure you that your expertise will be a blessing to someone else. My current parish, for instance, does not have a feeding garden the way my last parish did. But we have found other ways for the talented gardeners in our midst to connect to others who might need their guidance. When the church building was shut down during the pandemic, we hosted online garden chats, with people taking turns giving short talks about their favorite gardening topic. We also became connected to a feeding garden at a nearby Methodist church, sending volunteers there and raising money for them during the Easter season. Two of their lead gardeners showed up at our Zoom coffee hour, and we shared a short video so that people could see what a beautiful and inviting place their garden was. This helped establish connections between our two congregations, connections we hope to continue to build on.

There is one final example of how community is built in a garden that I'd like to share, and it brings us full circle to the topic of soil. Alongside pursuing our theme of "Healthy Soil, Healthy Plants, Healthy Communities," the creation care team at my parish in Davis began to invite speakers from local indigenous communities to teach us about their relationship with the land. We have called this series Seeds of Justice, and it has really been like seeds, sprouting new ideas and relationships at every turn. We also took a field trip to a nearby "tending and gathering garden," an area situated in a former gravel mining pit where indigenous methods of land restoration are being practiced, as well as taught to younger generations.

While on this field trip, we learned that a large new mining site was being proposed in the area, basically neighboring a nature conservancy, on land that is currently used for agriculture. This new mining project is in my hometown, but I knew nothing about it until I began making these connections with the individuals and groups who are advocating for indigenous environmental practices and land restoration in our region. Since that field trip, several of us have become involved in efforts to get our county to slow and eventually stop the spread of new mining projects, which are at odds with many of our stated environmental goals.

So far, we have not succeeded in our efforts to stop mining. But I do know that we have raised public awareness about some of the hidden costs to our community, including the loss of acres and acres of topsoil. It has also inspired many of us to become involved in local politics like never before, meeting with members of our Board of Supervisors, attending and commenting at public meetings, writing letters to the editor, and more. While there was a time not so long ago that the issue of soil health, and especially its link to carbon sequestration, would have meant nothing to me, gardening was the gateway to opening my mind and heart to these critical issues. It has also been the gateway to my parish becoming more connected to the larger community, in ways that make us all stronger and healthier. The soil needs a voice, an advocate, and our community is stepping up to that role.

It is both a practical and a spiritual imperative that we recognize the incredible complexity of soil, this most common and fundamental material. Treating soil like dirt means having an extractivist attitude, taking and taking without recognizing its limits, keeping it on artificial life support with chemical treatments and fertilizers, and then abandoning it when it is no longer useful to you and letting it dry up and blow away. On the other hand, if you feed soil with rich organic matter and treat it with respect, it will reward you with abundant harvests and will both live itself and create and sustain new life basically forever.

The same can be said for our relationships, whether with plants, animals, or other human beings. People, like plants, as Ragan Sutterfield writes, "need to live in multicultural spaces of dependence—varied life is what gives us health."[13]

Discussion Questions

1. What stands out to you about the distinction between dirt and soil?

2. How does understanding soil as a living web of relationships expand our definition of community?
3. What is the connection between humility and gratitude?
4. What does the Three Sisters garden have to say about the nature of our connectedness?
5. How does gardening make us less alone?

CHAPTER FOUR

DEATH AND COMPOST: LEARNING TO LOVE OUR LIMITS

Credit: iStock.com/Jurgute

Gardens are happy places. There are more and more studies and books coming out about how gardening is good for our emotional and physical health, something that gardeners have known since time immemorial. Telling us that gardening is good for us is like telling us that we're better off having access to oxygen. Does it even need to be said?

When we garden we practice hope, putting our faith in nature's ability to bring forth life, to create something beautiful and nourishing from the modest ingredients of soil, seeds, and time. In other words, gardens are places of health, hope, and healing. And yet, it would also be true to say that gardens are places of death, decay, and failure. These two truths go hand in hand.

Anyone who has gardened for more than a season or two is likely to have stories of epic failure, of whole crops destroyed by blight or insects, of a favorite tree that was healthy and productive one summer and dead the next, of a singularly persistent inability to grow roses. If people who fish are known for their tendency to exaggerate their successes, I've noticed that people who garden are more likely to talk about their failures. It's not universally true, of course, but humility is a common trait among gardeners I know. Sometimes it feels like more than mere humility—almost like they dwell on the negatives. A friend of mine is typical. She was always talking about everything that was going wrong in her garden, so much so that I was astonished when I first visited and saw it was a place of lush delight, simply brimming with healthy plants. It wasn't that she was unaware of how well most of her garden was doing, she told me, but rather that she didn't pay as much attention to the plants that were thriving. "They don't need me—they're perfectly happy," she said. "It's the struggling ones I feel responsible for."

It used to puzzle me that gardens can contain so much that reminds us of life's limitations—plants that die too young, landscaping plans that fail, fruit trees with dismal yields—and yet can still be places that are so rewarding and downright good for us. Now I think that is part of their appeal. Perhaps what is really soul-satisfying and conducive to deep happiness, even joy, isn't what we think it is. From pop culture, the media, and especially advertising we soak up the message that what we want, what will make us happy, is endless sunshine, perfect physical bodies and shiny white teeth, getting everything we work for or even simply wish for. Gardening comes with no guarantee of success, with an inescapable reliance on the weather, with aching knees, grubby clothes, and sunburned noses, and with the possibility that, when all is said and done, we'll have very little to show for a lot of labor. Gardening requires us to confront the uncomfortable reality that we are not in control of most of the circumstances of our life and that, what's more, all of life comes to an end, sometimes sooner rather than later. And yet somehow, for many of us, that comes as a blessed relief. It's as if we are starving for the truth, for the real nourishment it gives us, and all around we find cotton-candy fantasies instead.

I once heard a fascinating interview with the author of a book that compared two styles of parenting, using the metaphor of parents as either carpenters or gardeners. I knew immediately what she was getting at. Carpenters plan, measure, and construct with a specific outcome in mind; while gardeners *may* also plan, measure, and construct, we must of necessity be much more flexible and adaptive as to the specific outcome of our work. Botany is a science, but gardening is an art—and a spiritual practice, of course.

Don't misunderstand me. Someone could write a book about carpentry as a spiritual practice and I'd be eager to read it. My younger daughter finds beauty in mathematics and thinks computer science is a creative endeavor, because it is, or it certainly can be. Life is not a competition to determine which activities are more intrinsically beautiful, artistic, or spiritual. Our spirits can be fed and formed by almost any pursuit that brings us joy and satisfaction. But the lessons learned through hours spent writing computer code are different from the lessons learned in a garden, and they will shape us in different ways.

While people often talk about their gardens as a place of refuge or escape, I'd offer that it's more about escaping *to* reality than escaping from reality. What we'll explore more in this chapter is how the garden's lessons are not all sweetness and light but rather provide an avenue into the issues of death, limitation, imperfection, and other topics that are so often taboo in our culture and that we secretly long to face.

Death, Compost, and Returning to Dust

Death is the ultimate limit, the one entirely unavoidable reality of life. No matter how much you accomplish, how much money you make, how smart or good-looking you are, how saintly, how powerful, none of that makes an iota of difference when it comes to the inevitability of death. I'm going to die. You're going to die. Everyone we love is going to die. I won't belabor the point any more than I already have, but I think it's worth being blunt and stating (and restating) the obvious when it comes to the topic of death, because the world around us seems hell-bent on making sure we don't talk about it at all. Denial of death is the name of the game, especially in a media environment that is still trying to sell us on the idea that whoever has the most toys wins and that staying young and healthy forever is entirely possible for the price of a new shampoo, another cruise in the Caribbean, or membership at the neighborhood gym.

Sometimes people think that Christians are obsessed with death, or at least with life after death. In my experience, Christians are as avoidant about death as anyone else. And in Christian denominations like my own that have mostly stopped preaching about heaven and hell, it's even more likely that we won't discuss "what happens next" on a regular basis. There's been a course correction in biblical scholarship, and pastors and preachers in mainline churches are getting on board with the understanding that many passages we once believed to be about heaven and hell probably aren't that at all. The writers of the Bible, from the Old Testament prophets to the four or more fellows who wrote the Gospels, were much more interested in what happens in this life than the next, if they even believed in an afterlife. There is a good side to this shift: scaring people into following Jesus by threatening them with eternal damnation if they don't follow your rules or believe in your version of God is a perversion of faith. It is a toxic and abusive form of religion.

On the other hand, what is the point of a faith that avoids any real grappling with big questions like what happens after we die? Surely there is a happy medium, a perspective that is neither threatening nor avoidant, that faces the reality of death squarely without using it as an excuse to enforce a narrow concept of acceptable beliefs and behavior.

Remember in a previous chapter when we talked about the *givens* of life, and how gardening can help us embrace reality? Death is one of the primary givens, and it is everywhere evident in a garden. While I don't know that gardening has actually so transformed me that I no longer fear death, it has helped me in the work of coming to terms with its reality.

In the Episcopal Church and many other denominations, we follow a liturgical calendar, a cycle of seasons and holy days in which each has its own character and focus. Some are familiar to the larger culture, such as Christmas and Easter. Some are more obscure: Ascensiontide, for instance, is probably not a word that means much to the average American—or even the average Episcopalian. (For the record, it's the ten-day period between Ascension Day and the feast of Pentecost. Aren't you glad you asked?) Other religions also follow a cyclical calendar, often mirroring in some way the natural cycle of seasons in the place where they originated. Growing up in Hawaii, I didn't have a very deep understanding of how important seasons could be; when I moved to Scotland during my junior year abroad, my eyes were opened to the realities of hunkering down in winter, reawakening in spring, and so on. Having rituals that connect you more deeply to the cyclical nature of life, whether arising from a faith tradition or connected to your work in a garden, can be a centering and grounding practice.

The season of Lent begins with Ash Wednesday and concludes just before Easter, which is the high point of the liturgical year. Lent is a season of repentance and preparation, of getting our spiritual house in order. In the words of the Book of Common Prayer, we are invited to observe this season "by self-examination and repentance; by prayer, fasting, and self-denial; and by reading and meditating on God's holy Word." Most of us associate Lent with the "fasting and self-denial" part; if you grew up Catholic or with a lot of Catholic friends, the question "What are you giving up for Lent?" was an annual ritual, not unlike asking, "What do you want for Christmas?"

When we gather in church on Ash Wednesday, it is with the express purpose of being reminded that we are going to die. This probably sounds morbid and potentially even a little obscene to an outside observer. Many within the church also resist the focus on death and "mortification of the flesh," to use another old-fashioned term. I remember reading a blog by a pastor who said that he never tells his flock to fast on Ash Wednesday but instead makes it an occasion to go out for ice cream after church. While well intentioned, such assertions by a leader of a congregation make me sad. I can go out for ice cream any day; how often can I count on someone to be honest, loving, and brave while helping me come to terms with mortality?

The centerpiece of the Ash Wednesday services is the imposition of ashes: people line up to have a priest or other minister draw a smudgy, ashy sign of the cross on their forehead and intone the words "Remember that you are dust, and to dust you shall return." The ashes are usually mixed with a little oil and will stay on your face all day or until you choose to wash them off. They are what people in an earlier age would have called a memento mori, a reminder of death. And, intriguingly, many people who are not regular churchgoers love this ritual and show up for it year after year, either in church services or when "ashes to go" are offered on street corners, at bus stops, in shopping malls, and just about anywhere else where busy people can stop for a moment and feel another person's hand on their shoulder and hear words that are both starkly truthful and oddly comforting.

As discussed in Chapter One, the story we commonly call the Fall takes place after the second creation myth in Genesis; it encompasses everything that happens from the moment Eve eats the forbidden fruit through the time the first human beings are banished from the Garden of Eden. It is within this story that we find the famous phrase "you are dust, and to dust you shall return." Adam and Eve, naked and ashamed, learn of the consequences of their actions. For one thing, they will have to work the fields in order to eat; this introduces an element of friction to their relationship with the created order. Even more ominously, they now learn of their mortality:

> By the sweat of your face
> you shall eat bread
> until you return to the ground,
> for out of it you were taken;
> you are dust,
> and to dust you shall return. (Genesis 3:19)

Given that in the Christian context this story is so often interpreted in terms of sin, disobedience, and punishment, it is no wonder that we hear these words as ominous and even threatening. Worse yet, it seems to set up an eternal enmity between human beings and the natural world. Now, if it were only a conflict between people and snakes, I could probably live with that—like Indiana Jones, I am terrified of snakes. Instead, though, the story of the Fall has been used to explain a division or even antagonism between human beings and all the rest of the created order, leading many to believe that nature red in tooth and claw is out to get us. It's true that this story *can* be read as being about divine punishment, but really it has more to do with grappling with why there is so much suffering and disharmony in the world. The story is a mirror, affirming that the often difficult and sometimes beautiful circumstances we face are real: life is short, we work hard, there is no escaping death, we're all made of the same stuff.

Just as gardening teaches us to reimagine how we understand words like "dirt" and "soil," it can also help us reframe the idea that we are made of "dust" and that we must work the land for our food. Believing that we are in competition for nature's scarce resources has driven a wedge between people and our environment and allowed us to make excuses for exploitation, domination, and an extractivist mindset, with all the attendant horrific consequences to the planet on which we all depend for life. Gardens teach us something else. We can work in cooperation with nature, as a partner, not a rival. It's still work, certainly, but that's okay. The better we treat the land, the better the land treats us; it's symbiotic, mutually supportive and nurturing. Sometimes when people teach the Three Sisters garden system, they remind students that we gardeners are the fourth sister, doing our own part to aid the corn, squash, and beans in their growth and flourishing.

A few years ago, we moved into a new house, with a flat and sunny backyard that I knew would make for some great gardening. It was June when we moved and my birthday is in July, so I told my family I only wanted one thing for my birthday: a compost bin. And not the cheap, slatted wooden containers that we'd had in past gardens; I wanted a proper, heavy-duty composter, a tumbler with different sections that you could spin regularly to help speed the process by which kitchen scraps are turned into black gold. And if they wanted to buy me some manure fertilizer or worm castings, even better.

Luckily my family no longer thinks twice about such odd gift requests. At my last parish I was dubbed "Compost Queen" because I was so enthusiastic about the stuff. It still feels like magic to me, the alchemy that takes cast-off organic material—what we call "waste"—and breaks it down into humus, the very best ingredient for helping plants grow. There is something so beautiful in taking what is unwanted and making it a sought-after, life-giving substance: who doesn't want to be part of the process of creating treasure from trash, life from death, abundance from decay? Could there be anything more miraculous than knowing that invisible microbes, bacteria, and fungi are feasting on what we have thrown away, and in return are giving us the very most basic *stuff* we need to continue eating and living?

The biologist and writer Merlin Sheldrake began marveling over this dance of life and death much earlier than I did. In his book *The Entangled Life*, he tells of how playing in leaf piles as a child led to his first experiments with decomposition. His father helped him observe worms wending their way through layers of leaves and soil, explaining that worms are just the creatures that we can see doing the work of decomposition, but that there are many more creatures, invisible to us, that "are able to mix and stir and dissolve one thing into another." He writes:

> Composers make pieces of music. These were decomposers, who unmake pieces of life. Nothing could happen without them. . . . Composers make; decomposers unmake. And unless decomposers unmake, there isn't anything that the composers can make *with*. It was a thought that changed the way I understood the world.[1]

These decomposers are at home in the soil, and they are what allow us—gardeners—to become composers. It's all connected. Thinking about compost and soil this way does not take away all the fear or sting of death, but it does gently ask me to reconsider my feelings about my own mortality, and my own materiality. Soil and I aren't so different. Like soil, I am made up of countless numbers of microscopic beings that use me as a host and that have become part of my biological reality, my microbiome. Soil needs compost, needs death, in order to create new life. Is that not true for people, as well? And not only at the literal level, in that our environment would be uninhabitable if nothing ever decomposed. More than that, I know that there are things in my life that need to die in order for me to embrace new possibilities. I have so much baggage that I must release, unburden myself of, if I want to keep growing, adapting, truly living. But that doesn't mean that there is any part of me, ever, that needs to be treated like dirt. Or any part of you, either.

Getting Dirty

Jesus seems to have been comfortable with dirt. I suppose he might have had no choice, living as he did in a dusty, sandy place without access to indoor plumbing. There is more to it than that, though. Jesus was comfortable with bodies, even unhealthy or unwholesome ones. In my Christian understanding of him as the most truly human person to ever live, I like to think that he wasn't put off by all our human messiness, whether of body or of spirit, and that the inherent messiness of nature wouldn't have bothered him, either.

One well-known episode from the New Testament that has always intrigued me is when Jesus is confronted by a group of religious leaders, upright and godly men in his community, who ask him what they should do with a woman they believe has committed adultery. To our modern ears, it sounds like there is a lot wrong with this scenario, including that the other party to the adultery (presumably a married man) is not mentioned. The verbal response of Jesus has become a famous aphorism, but it is the nonverbal response that fascinates me. According to the Gospel of John:

> The scribes and the Pharisees brought a woman who had been caught in adultery; and making her stand before all of them, they said to him, "Teacher, this woman was caught in the very act of committing adultery. Now in the law Moses commanded us to stone such women. Now what do you say?" They said this to test him, so that they might have some charge to bring against him. Jesus bent down and wrote with his finger on the ground. When they kept on questioning him, he straightened up and said to them, "Let anyone among you who is without sin be the first to throw a stone at her." And once again he bent down and wrote on the ground. When they heard it, they went away, one by one, beginning with the elders. (John 8:3–9)

Commentaries always want to know what it was that Jesus was writing while he avoided answering the trick question, but that has never been my focus. What grabs me about this passage is that Jesus was scribbling in the dirt. It is probably going too far to wonder if, like me, Jesus was also an inveterate mud-pie maker when he was a little kid. Regardless, he is unfussy enough to not hesitate to doodle in sand or dirt when that is what he has on hand. We don't know if Jesus ever had a garden of his own to tend, since at least as an adult he was mostly itinerant. But, like a lot of gardeners, he would have had dirt under his nails, and he would never judge us for our tendency to be a little disheveled or grubby. All those portraits hanging in church basements of Jesus with glowing skin and long shiny hair miss the mark entirely. Grubby Jesus is much more the kind of savior I can get behind.

While we are talking about Jesus and dirt, there is one other story we have to look at, this one from the very next chapter of John's Gospel. In this passage, Jesus and his disciples come across a man who has been blind from birth, and the disciples ask about the cause of his blindness. In keeping with the common understanding of that time, the disciples assume that this disability must have been the result of sin, either the man's own or that of his parents (the parents, presumably, are brought into it because the man was born blind—if he had lost his sight as an adult, the question of his parents might not have arisen). The Gospel continues:

> Jesus answered, "Neither this man nor his parents sinned; he was born blind so that God's works might be revealed in him. We must work the works of him who sent me while it is day; night is coming when no one can work. As long as I am in the

> world, I am the light of the world." When he had said this, he spat on the ground and made mud with the saliva and spread the mud on the man's eyes, saying to him, "Go, wash in the pool of Siloam." . . . Then he went and washed and came back able to see. (John 9:1–7)

There are some truly difficult theological issues here, such as whether God would choose to make a person blind from birth in order to give Jesus the chance to heal him (which is one interpretation of the phrase "so that God's works might be revealed") and what it means that "night is coming when no one can work." Setting those aside for someone more qualified to answer, I want us to focus on Jesus making mud and using it as an agent of healing.

Within the Gospel, this healing sets off a controversy among the religious authorities that is perhaps the firestorm they were trying to ignite when they brought the adulterous woman to him in the previous chapter. What is primarily so astonishing to all those who learn of the healing is that sight was given to one who had never had it: "Never since the world began has it been heard that anyone opened the eyes of a person born blind" (John 9:32). This leads the religious authorities to question not only the man but also his parents, all with the purpose of finding out what kind of person this Jesus is that he can perform this miracle. Still, even with the bigger issue of a miraculous healing and the questions about the source of Jesus's power being uppermost in the narrative, the use of mud continues to be included in descriptions of the event.

Why did Jesus make mud, using dirt and his own saliva, to use in healing this man? The short answer is that we don't know. There are many, many stories in the Gospels that show Jesus healing people without any such substance to assist him; sometimes he doesn't even need to touch the person or be physically present with them. Still, there is something so evocative about the use of mud. It seems to harken back in some way to God creating human beings from the soil, especially since Jesus positions this healing as a way of doing God's works in the world—and the religious authorities specifically want to disprove his association with God. There is also the fascinating detail that after he covers the man's eyes with the mud, Jesus instructs the man to go wash it off, and only then is his sight restored. To me, this speaks of something that I have learned as a gardener: the sense that the best things come when we are working in harmony with nature and God. The man is being given agency, a role to play in his own healing. This is what gardening feels like to me—a collaboration that includes creation, the Creator, and me, the creature, a collaboration that is like a dance in which we each have our own role to play, our own moment to shine, our own creative spark to add. And when it is going well, we almost forget that there are multiple dancers, and it just all feels like one beautiful movement. Jesus uses the natural materials at hand, and his own body, and the divine spirit that lived within him, and gave the man back both his sight and his dignity.

****

On Ash Wednesday I find myself drawn to remember what glorious and miraculous things God does with dust, with dirt, both in our stories and in our gardens. God the Creator took a little dust and blew the breath of life into it, making the first human being. Jesus used a little dust (and his own spit) to bring the gift of sight to a blind man. Garden soil is thought to have microbes in it that improve mental health as well as physical health. Nothing sums up my feelings about soil better than the quote "Essentially, all life depends upon the soil. . . . There can be no life without soil and no soil without life; they have evolved together."[2] And yet that soil would not be possible without death, decay, and decomposition. I will never get over the beauty and wonder of this.

I've been a priest for over a decade now, and I have not tired of the annual ritual of imposing ashes on people and reciting those words, "Remember you are dust, and to dust you shall return." I have said these words to strangers, students on a nearby college campus who stopped at our Ashes to Go table, and to my own husband and children. I have traced that sign of the cross on the faces of babies so young they could not possibly understand my words, and on the faces of terminally ill people who knew they were entering their very last season of Lent. The vulnerability and trust people exhibit when they tip their faces toward me, sometimes holding back hair, almost always closing their eyes, takes my breath away. It is such a privilege to be the person who bears that message, the person people trust to tell them the truth.

When I look around a church on Ash Wednesday, or a garden any day of the year, and remind myself that we are all dust, I know in my bones that I do not need to feel fear or shame. I am in good company. God made this dust, after all, and pronounced it very good. We are, in a phrase, beloved dust.

Ugly Vegetables: Imperfection and the Garden

Gardens are gloriously imperfect places. That is one of their gifts to us—they require us to let go of our dreams of perfection if we are ever going to find enjoyment in them.

When I first started growing fruits and vegetables as part of our church garden project, I was sometimes a . . . surprised by how they looked. There was so much anticipation and excitement around watching seeds sprout and plants grow that when they finally began to produce harvestable crops I was like a proud parent ready to show off my first child to the world. Nobody had warned me that some of my "offspring" might have looks that only a mother could love. There were carrots that were every shape imaginable except carrot-shaped, squash that looked like alien beings dropped to earth from a UFO, strawberries that were perfectly ripe but so small that they hardly seemed worth the effort to pick. Not to mention how often a row of plants would have stragglers or ne'er-do-wells—that one head of lettuce that just never quite fully formed into anything much, or the sugar snap pea plant that was half the height of its neighbors and we had no idea why, or the gorgeous tomato that you picked before discovering it had been partially eaten by some other creature already.

It turns out that there was nothing wrong with our garden or what we were growing. I, like most Americans who get our food from supermarkets, had become accustomed to unnaturally perfect produce. We want apples that are uniformly red and shiny, strawberries the size of golf balls, lettuce without a hint of wilt anywhere. We throw out anything that has a speck or a spot or a blemish—often before it even leaves the farm, because growers know how high (or how superficial) consumers' standards are. For several generations now, we have sacrificed taste and nutrition for food that looks good and holds up to travel, as our desire for out-of-season foods has caused much of our produce to be shipped long distances.

Credit: iStock.com/Katsiaryna Voitsik

Happily, the cultural tide is turning. Farmers, gardeners, and environmentalists are all teaching people about the problem of food waste in our country. They are also fighting back with humor and creativity, as certain outlets now proudly specialize in "ugly" or "misfit" foods. The local food movement has led to an explosion of interest in farmers' markets and community-supported agriculture programs. A growing awareness about the climate emergency we're in is also leading to a greater understanding that the massive scale of food waste in the United States is not just wasteful but hazardous to our planet's health. Composting helps keep some food out of the landfills, but it's not enough. Just as when it comes to other consumer products we have to reduce and reuse as well as recycle, we need to get more of the food grown from the farm or garden actually to the table, instead of thrown out before we even have a chance to compost the stuff we don't eat. In a country that grows more food than we need and yet where millions go hungry, the realization that perhaps as much as one-third of our food is thrown away is mind-boggling.[3]

Perfectionism doesn't just skew our perspective on food—it distorts the way we see ourselves and others. Our culture's obsession with superficial and narrow standards of what is attractive is insidious and does real damage to the mental health and well-being of too many of us who internalize these unrealistic, airbrushed standards and always feel like we're a disappointment by comparison. Add to that multiple other unrealistic and unhealthy pressures around achievement and acquisition (having a "good" job, a big house, fancy vacations, the newest gadgets, and so on), and you have a toxic setup for people to feel always behind, always falling short, always failing in one way or another.

Gardens are an antidote to all that striving and worry. While I'm convinced that nobody ever has created the perfect garden, every garden is good enough. Even homely vegetable gardens, my personal favorite, offer beautiful colors, rich fragrances, and other aesthetic pleasures, not to mention yummy food to eat. The act of gardening takes me out of myself, out of my head, and out of the dark places where I worry endlessly about whether I am a good enough mother, a good enough priest, a good enough friend, daughter, and so on. In a garden, my efforts always feel good enough. Not because every plant thrives and produces perfect fruit or a social-media-ready tableau, but because with enough time and effort something good will come of it. Not necessarily what I expected or intended, but something good nonetheless.

The physical nature of gardening is part of what makes it so beneficial in countering worry and perfectionism. Although you might not know it by watching some lifestyle gurus on TV or the internet, gardening is grubby, messy, sweaty work. It's best done in old clothes and floppy, usually unflattering hats. Your garden absolutely does not care what you look like. Gardens are great places to let off steam, to talk to yourself or to your plants, to forget about your phone, to experiment and play, and to remember what it feels like to be a kid running through sprinklers on a hot summer afternoon. After even an hour of work in the garden I feel justified in skipping the gym and spending the next half hour lying on the grass watching clouds instead.

When my husband and I were getting married, I was a student at Harvard Divinity School, and I had a lot of ideas about what a great marriage ceremony should be, how to make it theologically rich as well as aesthetically pleasing. Nearly thirty years later, I am not proud of the dresses I picked out for my bridesmaids, but I am incredibly grateful for the Scripture passage I chose. It was the portion of the Sermon on the Mount that reads in part:

> Therefore I tell you, do not worry about your life, what you will eat or what you will drink, or about your body, what you will wear. Is not life more than food, and the body more than clothing? Look at the birds of the air; they neither sow nor reap nor gather into barns, and yet your heavenly Father feeds them. . . . Consider the lilies of the field, how they grow; they neither toil nor spin, yet I tell you, even Solomon in all his glory was not clothed like one of these. So do not worry about tomorrow, for tomorrow will bring worries of its own. Today's trouble is enough for today. (Matthew 6:25–29, 34)

Without doubt, I could add, "Look at the tomato plants, at those beautiful climbing beans, at the cucumber vine that is making its merry way across the garden path. They do not have bank accounts, or retirement funds, or Twitter followers. And yet they are beloved and fruitful and more than good enough."

At the same time that the garden allows us an escape from the harsher pressures of life, I do not think it is an escape from reality. Rather, as I have said, it is an escape *to* reality. In the garden I confront not only my silly anxieties and competitiveness, which are fairly easily set aside, but some of my shadow side as well: my laziness and impatience, my discomfort with silence and solitude. Some garden work is repetitive and just plain boring. My resistance to going out to the garden when it is too hot or too buggy, or when I'm not in the mood and have other things I'd rather do, can also teach me a lot about myself.

In the day-to-day busyness of life, it can be hard to see myself clearly enough so that I can begin to get out of my own way, can start recognizing the obstacles standing between me and a more intimate relationship with the land, with God, and with other people. This is a kind of refining fire that many of us fear. It can be painful, it can be heartbreaking, and I wonder if sometimes our focus on doing, even on doing good work and good deeds, can be a way to avoid this introspective clarity. At such times, being in the garden reminds me that God loves all that God has made—all of us, no exceptions. No one of us is so flawed that God cannot do great things with us, no one of us so insignificant that God cannot use us to do infinitely more than we can ask or imagine.

Several years ago, I purchased an icon of the face of Christ. It was hand-painted with great care and skill, and it's very beautiful, with lots and lots of gold, and in it Christ looks both radiant and sad, both human and divine. I proudly brought it back to my office and pinned it up on the wall, but, not being very good at that sort of thing, I didn't do it properly. After only a few minutes of hanging there it came crashing down to my desk. The fall did some serious damage. Now the icon has a big chunk missing from its frame, as well as a bit of gold paint missing from around the upraised hand of Christ. When I first saw the damage, my heart sank. I thought that having a broken and flawed icon would drive me crazy, but the truth is, it hasn't. After all, in it I can still see Jesus. His face is still radiant and still sad, his hand is still raised in blessing, He is still loving me and seeking me more ardently than I will ever be able to love and seek him.

Seeing that chipped, flawed, and yet still radiant icon reminds me to look on myself and others with more gentleness and grace. We do not have to hide our flaws from God or one another. We do not have to pursue martyrdom or suffering, any more than we have to pursue perfection. We do not have to work at being good enough so that God will finally love us. God already loves us, and so we only need to seek to respond to that love by offering ourselves, our souls and our bodies, back to the world. A garden is a great place to start.

The Wisdom of Seeds

Several years ago, my family and I walked around a boarded-up area of St. Louis that had become a flashpoint for clashes between police and protesters after the death of Michael Brown, a young unarmed black man shot by police in the suburb of Ferguson. We were there that day to show our support for local businesses and for a community that was undergoing intense trauma. After windows had been smashed and then boarded up, local artists had come in and painted the plywood, so the whole neighborhood was like a pop-up art installation. It was both heartbreaking and beautiful. One of the signs I remember most vividly read, "They thought they had buried us. They didn't know we were seeds."

I've seen this slogan many times since then, and it always makes me stop and take notice. Seeds are a metaphor for growth and potential; to a gardener, a seed packet you can buy for a dollar in the hardware store represents a whole world of possibility. To the untrained eye, some seeds are so small they almost look like specks of dirt; nearly all seeds we commonly sow in a garden are visually unassuming, giving no indication of the vitality hidden inside.

Jesus compares himself to a seed. "Unless a grain of wheat falls into the earth and dies," he says, "it remains just a single grain; but if it dies, it bears much fruit" (John 12:24). Notice that according to this metaphor, Jesus is not just any seed, but a grain of wheat. Jesus also told his followers that he was the bread of life. He is explaining that in order for that bread to become available to the world, to truly become bread to nourish the whole world, he will first have to die. Going back again to our human tendency to want to avoid the topic of death, we won't be surprised that Jesus's followers were resistant to his message, as many of us continue to be today, if we're honest.

The wisdom of seeds and those who tend them can teach us lessons that are not readily available in our culture. They teach us that too often we look in the wrong places for hope and solace. We look to people and things that are big and bright, loud and assertive. Seeds are none of those things. Seeds are small, noiseless, and seemingly insignificant. They can be crushed underfoot, tossed aside, ground down. And yet it is in these acts that their true power is released. Seeds work underground, in the dark, sending out tendrils of new life in secret, often sprouting in unexpected and even inhospitable places. Seeds are the essence of resilience.

There is a story that medieval Christians liked to tell that has come down to us through artwork and poetry. It is not a story we find in the Bible, just to be clear. It goes something like this.

When Adam, as in Adam and Eve, was nearing the end of his life, he sent his son Seth back to the Garden of Eden on an errand. The archangel Michael, now guarding the entrance to the Garden, gave Seth a single seed to carry back home. This seed was one that had fallen from the Tree of the Knowledge of Good and Evil, the tree under which Seth's parents had disobeyed God. After Adam died and just before he was buried, Seth placed the seed in Adam's mouth. From it grew a tree—a barren tree that produced neither leaves nor fruit.

Eventually the tree was cut down and used to build a bridge. The bridge was later dismantled, but through a series of miraculous events the wood that came from the bridge that came from the tree that came from the seed that came from the Garden of Eden ended up being the very wood that was used, many generations later, to build the cross upon which Jesus was crucified. There are a number of legends about what happened to the wood of the cross after Jesus was taken down from it, far too many to tell here. My favorite end to this story is one suggested by medieval iconography that sometimes depicts the wood of the cross becoming a tree again—this time, the Tree of Life that is located in the center of the heavenly Jerusalem. As depicted in the book of Revelation, this tree sits "on either side of the river" of life, "and the leaves of the tree are for the healing of the nations" (Revelation 22:2).

The world needs an awful lot of healing right now. We have lived through some very dark and difficult times and they are not over yet. But seeds remind us that darkness is not always cause for despair; it might be where growth is happening. The resilience of seeds reminds us to keep hope alive. Keep faith alive. Keep love alive. As it says in the book of the prophet Isaiah, "For as rain and snow come down from heaven and do not return there until they have watered the earth, making it bring forth and sprout, giving seed to the sower and bread to the eater, so shall my word be that goes out from my mouth; it shall not return to me empty, but it shall accomplish that which I have purposed, and succeed in the thing for which I sent it"(Isaiah 55:10–11). Seeds are a sign of promise.

If we truly want to find goodness, even divinity, in the world, we can. We can see it in communities that come together to garden, to reach out to others in need, and to care for one another, even in the midst of anxious and uncertain times. We can see it wherever we see people being resilient, rising from the ashes of hate and prejudice, of violence and dehumanization. We can see it in the tiny seeds of faith and love that people plant in our hearts with every act of kindness, generosity, and solidarity. We can even see it in boarded-up shop windows given new life and meaning with vibrant, colorful, hope-filled works of art.

Discussion Questions

1. How does coming to terms with our limitations open our lives to greater freedom?

2. How does coming to terms with death enhance our living?
3. How does perfection keep us from expressing our true selves?
4. What do you feel when you think of yourself as a seed?

CHAPTER FIVE

HOSPITALITY AND JUSTICE: WHOSE LAND IS IT, ANYWAY?

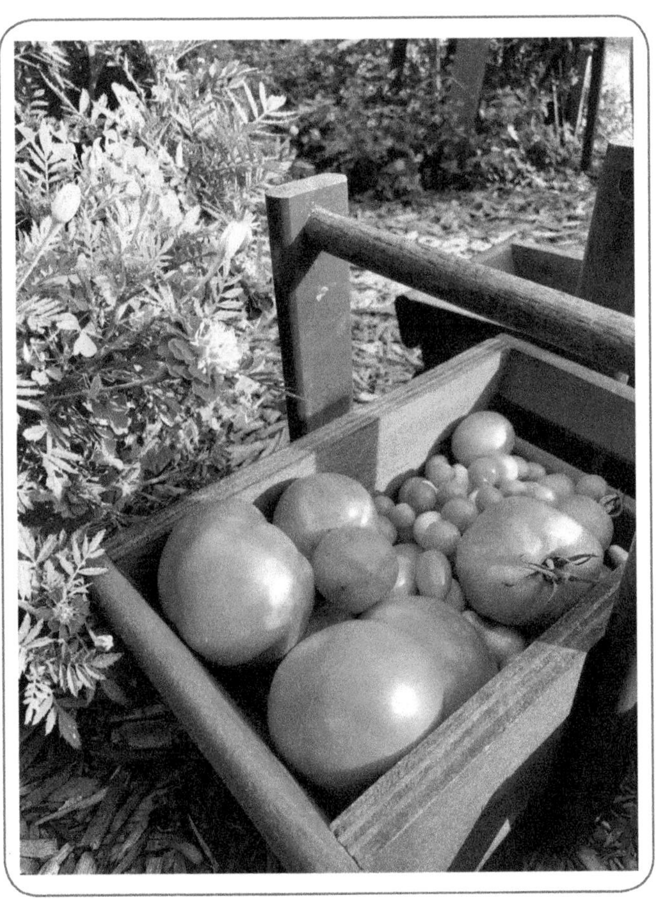

We've already looked a little at how gardens can build community, using the rich metaphor of soil as our starting point. In this chapter, we'll expand that vision even more, into the areas of hospitality and justice work. Let's start by imagining a picnic table laden with food. It sits under the shade of an oak tree, offering welcome, comfort, and abundance on a warm late summer evening.

What food do you envision on that table? As a vegetarian and a gardener, I see a spinach salad with heirloom tomatoes, creamy avocados, and chunks of salty feta; a quinoa-based dish with pomegranate seeds and walnuts and a citrus dressing; lots of warm, crusty sourdough bread; some roasted veggies; and of course a dessert featuring summer fruit, probably blackberries served in meringue boats with a dollop of crème fraîche and a sprinkling of brown sugar. (I'm making myself hungry thinking about it.) Are these foods in season? Can they be grown where you live?

Next, I wonder who is sitting around the table. Is it just close friends or family? What if you were to invite neighbors or community members—how well do you know the people who live around you? Or maybe it's an affinity group of some kind: other gardeners, or a knitting circle or book club, or people from your local church or synagogue or mosque. Do the people all look alike, in terms of ethnicity, age range, race, and so on? How would you make room for strangers, or even just for people very different from you? When I imagine this table welcoming people from my church, I know that the majority would fit within a certain narrow demographic, an older, mostly white, mostly well-educated bunch. But there would also be the new couple who joined our church during the pandemic lockdown, when we were online only, and whose baby we recently baptized; another family with four young kids, all of whom are seeking asylum in the United States after fleeing their war-torn homeland in Central America and have been part of our community for three years now; a student from the nearby university who is trying to figure out how their shifting sense of gender identity fits with their Christian faith. How much room is at your table for people significantly different from you?

Where is the table located? Do you have a space where you live, work, or worship where you might be able to set up a table outside and invite others? If not, let your imagination roam—maybe this is a table at a nearby park or community garden, or a place you would like to go but haven't been to yet. Then begin to ask yourself what you know about that land. Who owns it and for how long has it been theirs? Was it ever used for other purposes? Where your church or synagogue or other worship space now stands, was there once an orchard, or a farm, or a field? Do you know where your water comes from, or anything about the health of your watershed? If you live in an area that experiences drought, as I do, have you considered how much water was needed to grow the food you're eating? What will be left on the table when the meal is over—plates, utensils, food scraps, napkins—and what will happen to it next?

My hope is that as we move through these layers of questions, the intimate connection between hospitality and justice is beginning to reveal itself. Gardening is a spiritual practice that moves us beyond the realm of the personal to a concern for the land on which we grow our food and the people who will eat it, whether they are other members of our household or people you might never meet who will access it through a food pantry where you donate your produce. From there it is almost impossible not to start thinking about why some people have access to gardens and some don't, why some people have healthful, fresh produce readily available to them and others live in food deserts, and so on.

Our ancestors in faith were clear that the cultivation of land has ethical implications. It would have been unthinkable for writers of the Bible to leave out the issue of land when considering how a community would make decisions about ownership, leadership, and the distribution of resources. The Old Testament scholar Ellen Davis has shown that a faithful reading of the Bible requires us to acknowledge the agrarian perspective of those who wrote it; she even goes so far as to say that their vision of "heaven and earth" was a close parallel to what ecologist Aldo Leopold famously called "the land community."[1] She includes in the basic elements of the Bible's "theological land ethic" these two assumptions: "that humans and land exist in a biotic unity before God [and] that their unity has identifiable moral dimensions (faithful action, truth, righteousness)."[2]

Gardening is the best option most of us have to get in touch with the land community; sorting out the moral and ethical dimensions of our gardens is urgent and necessary work in a world that is increasingly confronting issues around diversity, equity, and inclusion, not to mention the existential challenge of climate change. Our hospitality would be very superficial indeed if we were content to see some of our neighbors overfed while others go hungry, or if we refused to consider whether our gardening practices were good for the planet or detrimental to it.

With this chapter, we are entering into territory that can be uncomfortable and contentious, and I want to be clear that in most cases there aren't easy "right" and "wrong" answers to the quandaries we face. Entering into hard conversations with humility, with open hearts and minds, and with an assumption of good intentions on the part of our conversation partners (in this case, you the reader and I the author) will go a long way in making these productive, loving, and life-giving interactions.

Let me start with just one example of how questions of ethics and morality arise alongside gardening practices. When my last parish was first discussing starting a garden, we were offered a $10,000 grant to get Shepherd Farm off the ground. In the Episcopal Church, a substantial financial gift to a parish, especially one with strings attached, usually needs to be approved by the Vestry, the governing body of laypeople. When the grant for starting the garden was discussed by the leadership, someone asked a simple question that gave us all pause: "How many cans of beans could we buy for $10,000?"

There was no rancor in the question; rather it appeared to be motivated by a fair and reasonable desire for us to be rational and to do the math. If our stated purpose for the garden was to raise food to help feed hungry people, and we were willing to spend $10,000 to do that, shouldn't we consider how much more food we might be able to give away if we used the money to buy inexpensive, nonperishable canned goods? This question actually led to a thoughtful and productive discussion about the purpose of the garden. Our goal was to give produce to people who were food insecure, yes. But we wanted to look at *how* we were feeding the hungry, and *what* we were feeding them, not simply *how much* we could give away. Words like "relationship" and "connection" came to the forefront in that discussion; in the end there was general agreement that it would be a more personal and meaningful process to give away fresh food that we had grown ourselves rather than processed food we bought.

I can easily imagine another outcome, one where a community decided that their own spiritual growth and commitment to creation care were really beside the point, or at least secondary to the urgent needs of people in their neighborhood. That community's decision might be that they needed to get as many calories onto the plates of as many hungry people as they could, as quickly as possible. The answer in that case would have been to raise money and buy food, pronto. Would any of us really say that was wrong? And yet, had my parish gone that route, Shepherd Farm would never have been born. Different communities will have different resources available to them, different priorities, and different answers to the serious problems we all face. And that's just fine. What matters is that the questions are being asked and that hard conversations and real discernment are not being avoided as we seek to answer them. Part of the conversation needs to be about the difference between charity (i.e., feeding people) and justice (i.e., ensuring that people have the means and opportunity to feed themselves), a conversation that is still new to many faith communities.

Another example comes from Norman Wirzba in the book *Making Peace with the Land*. He tells the story of the Anathoth

Community Garden, an endeavor that grew out of an experience of violence that nearly shattered the small community of Cedar Grove, North Carolina. As people sought ways to reconcile after a beloved community member was murdered, one fifth-generation resident "received a vision from God that she should give five acres of land to help feed the hungry." As an African American descendant of sharecroppers, Scenobia Taylor was both the victim of years of racism and also a leader in the movement toward racial reconciliation. Using her land generously and productively was the strongest statement she could make and the most meaningful gift she could give. Wirzba records her as saying, "And then here we have all this land here. And then what we do with it? We not doin' nothin'. I wanted to do something like you know my grandfather and father did, you know. And I just pray, and I were praying and I said Lord, please show me, give me a sign or something.'"[3] Here we clearly see the intersection of issues of justice, race, land ownership and access, and how one avenue toward healing and wholeness for that community turned out to be growing food together.

Beyond Martha Stewart: Definitions of Hospitality

"Hospitality" is one of those words that needs no definition—until it does. Most often we use the word to refer to things like dinner parties or wedding receptions. In faith communities, there might be a "hospitality committee" that organizes coffee hours and potluck suppers. During the pandemic of 2020 and beyond, many of us have had to expand our understanding of hospitality, figuring out how to offer welcome and maintain relationships when we could not be together in person. Online gatherings, classes, prayer groups, and other opportunities to connect remotely (what an oxymoron) mushroomed overnight. And many of us found that the relative safety of outdoor activities made community gardening more popular than ever. I would like us to stretch our definition of hospitality even a little more.

In her chapter on hospitality in *Practicing Our Faith*, theologian Ana María Pineda defines hospitality as "the practice of providing a space where the stranger is taken in and known as one who bears gifts."[4] I hear in that the call to extend hospitality beyond the bounds of our own family or community and out to strangers, with the recognition that there is a mutuality implied in this form of hospitality: we who offer space are welcoming in others with gifts, from which we will learn or be enriched in some way. Writer Christine Pohl agrees, noting that many people today are likely to think of hospitality primarily as providing welcome and entertainment to those they know rather than in terms of opening their homes or even their parish halls to strangers. She writes, "For the most part, the term 'hospitality' has lost its moral dimension."[5]

For me, it was working in a church garden that awakened and developed my sense of the "moral dimension" of hospitality. Growing up, I had seen church as a place where I personally got to have an experience of meeting God, primarily through receiving communion. This was a wonderful thing, to be sure. But it mostly ignored the possibility, and the beauty, of meeting God in other people and the world around me, and perhaps of finding ways to open other people to an experience of God as well. We weren't the kind of family that usually stuck around for coffee hour or volunteered for a lot of activities; we liked to go to church, worship, maybe say hi to the pastor, and go home. But I'm not sure that more hours hanging around a church hall eating donuts would have made that much of a difference to my spirituality. Perhaps I simply wasn't ready sooner, or perhaps I needed the hospitality of the garden to open up this more expansive, receptive side of my spiritual life.

Norman Wirzba argues that it is in the nature of gardening to create hospitality with a moral and ethical center, because gardening is in God's nature (and God's nature is not only itself good but is the source of all goodness). The image of God as gardener, which he finds repeatedly in Scripture, reminds us that

> the divine creative activity is fundamentally about "making room" for others to be and to flourish. Garden work is a form of hospitality in which the focus is on the welcome and wellbeing of others. . . . Created in the image of God, humanity's highest calling is to witness to the hospitality that God first demonstrated in planting the world.[6]

"Making room" is one of my favorite metaphors for hospitality. It encompasses the multidimensional nature of garden hospitality: the land makes room for us, we make room on the land for a garden, and then the garden makes room for others. It's a veritable cycle of gracious hospitality involving people, land, and divine welcome.

Hospitality, as I understand it, is also about transformation. It should change us, or at least help us stay open to the possibility of being changed. The authors of a popular book on Benedictine hospitality wrote, "In human labor an astonishing thing happens: God shows up. As we prepare a place for others, something happens inside of us: we are prepared also."[7] This is a good reminder of how hospitality is important to the person offering it as well as to the person receiving it; it shouldn't be something we do *for* others but fundamentally something we do *alongside* or in companionship with others. The person or group offering hospitality needs to maintain enough humility in their practice to recognize that, at its best, hospitality is more mutual than one-sided. Pohl makes a similar observation: "Hospitality is good for everyone—good for hosts as well as for guests. The testimony of so many people who offer hospitality is that they 'received more than they gave.'"[8] This is one form that the change or transformation implicit in the practice can take: the person who offers hospitality can end up experiencing feelings of being welcome, fed, seen, and known.

Transformation, though, is not always easy. To be genuinely open to transformation, we must be willing to risk change and even loss. Again, a garden is a good teacher. While churches often talk about wanting to grow, we simultaneously tend to resist change. And yet what is growth if not change? That old bean seed experiment that so many schoolchildren are assigned—planting a seed in a see-through cup so you can witness how it evolves from seed to sprouting plant—should be proof enough, but so often we miss the point. Real growth cannot happen without change. Does a bean plant miss being a seed? I don't know, but I do know that we human beings have to grieve the things we leave behind, old habits and rituals and ways of thinking, even if they no longer serve us or they are standing in the way of our relationships and our ability to offer genuine hospitality.

I often think about a church I visited where it was very hard to find my way from the parking lot to the sanctuary. Following others who seemed to know what they were doing, I found myself walking through what appeared to be someone's dining room: there were a bunch of men sitting around a table drinking coffee, most of them with their backs to me. I scurried past, feeling awkward and intrusive, and eventually found my way to where the worship service was just starting. Later, I was able to ask a member of the church what exactly it was that I had stumbled across, and she explained that those were just some of the longtime members who liked to sit outside the church kitchen having a cup of coffee before the service began. She laughed. "Sometimes they sneak in a little late, because they are having such a good time catching up." It was an interesting moment: to those men, that little coffee circle was part of what made their parish feel like home; to me as a visitor, it felt like a signal that I was out of place and possibly not welcome. Should they have been willing to give up their beloved ritual to create a more welcoming environment for visitors? I imagine this would have felt like a terrible loss to them. This is one of those many instances where there isn't a right answer, but the conversation needs to happen if we want our communities to practice deep, generous hospitality.

Hospitality, viewed in this way, is also about expanding our circles of inclusivity. Gardens are wonderful for this because they tend to be easily accessible, existing in spaces that are socially permeable rather than fixed. Almost as soon as the Shepherd Farm garden began, parishioners who spent time working in it noticed that it created a new sense of belonging—not just belonging to the church, but also of feeling more like a part of our neighborhood. The lawn, which had been such

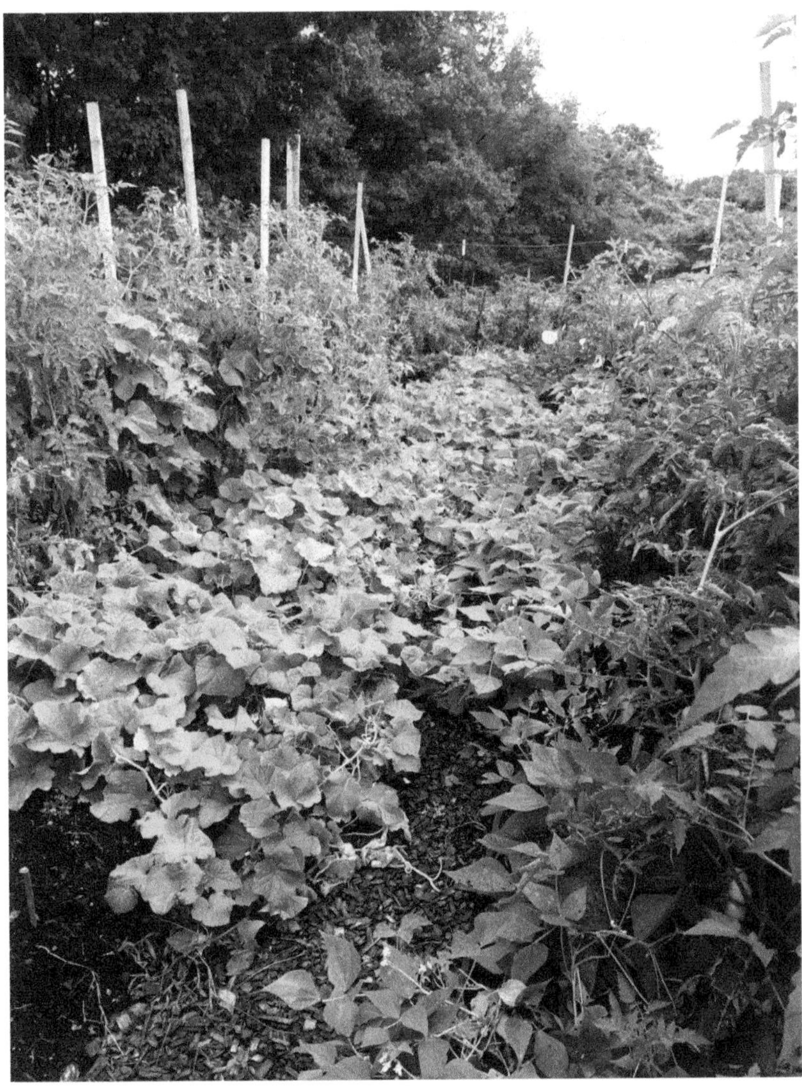

a seamless expanse of grass, now had a major feature on it, a focal point. The twin defenses of sameness and distance had been breached. Christine Pohl writes, "Hospitality begins at the gate, in the doorway, on the bridges between public and private space. Finding and creating threshold places is important for contemporary expressions of hospitality."[9] This is a key function for a garden at a church or other public place. It is exactly a "threshold" space, existing as it does on the property but not inside the building. It serves as a kind of bridge between the neighborhood and the faith community; we found repeatedly that people who lived nearby, who had never set foot in the church, were interested in getting to know those of us who were out working in the garden. Often they just stayed for a few minutes to hear about what we were growing or where we were donating the produce, but some stayed longer or became repeat visitors. It was especially gratifying when we could offer them tomatoes or green beans to take home with them as a small gesture of neighborliness.

We made room on our land for this garden, turned much of our focus to the welcome and well-being of others, and in the process received a steady stream of assurance that we were answering a calling that brought us closer to the heart of God. I've seen this happen at so many other churches as well, including the local Methodist church in the town where I now live; they host a wonderful ministry called Grace Garden that runs on the volunteer work of university students as well as other community members. The book *Harvesting Abundance: Local Initiatives of Food and Faith* by Brian Sellers-Petersen has more than a dozen examples of other Episcopal churches that have had great success with gardens and similar projects. Many more have come into existence since the book's publication in 2017; the Good News Garden movement has taken off exponentially since it began in 2020.[10]

This faith-based communal gardening movement is certainly not limited to Episcopal (and Methodist) churches. I recently attended a conference in California hosted by the Interfaith Sustainable Food Collaborative that featured speakers and participants from multiple faith traditions. One of my favorite panels featured a rabbi and an imam comparing and contrasting their traditions' food rules and practices. The Interfaith Sustainable Food Collaborative Facebook page says that it advances its mission by "connecting congregations with local farmers and gardeners to increase access to organic food and strengthen local economies; sharing models, strategies and resources across faith traditions to help leaders bring programs and best practices to their congregations, camps and retreat centers"; and much more. This is just one of many exciting examples of how faith communities can tap into gardening and related activities as a means to stretch their hospitality muscles, build community, and reach out to neighbors across divides that no longer seem so important in the face of our shared desire for a healthy planet and people. Hospitality as a spiritual practice finds a natural outlet in the garden, a place where people of different skills, abilities, temperaments, and even beliefs all have the opportunity to give, to receive, and to grow.

Making Room: From Contemplation to Action

One of the parishioners at my last church who was very involved in our garden, Shepherd Farm, told me a story that reminded me that the garden itself can be a hospitable place, apart from the people who work in it. Tina grew up in Iowa surrounded by farms and then spent her whole working life in the agricultural industry, but she was still surprised by how much working at Shepherd Farm has had an impact on her spiritual life and her sense of belonging in the parish. What surprised her most was that her sense of belonging is greatest when she spends time alone in the garden. She put it this way:

> Whether I'm out there with other people or whether I'm out there by myself, it's a different experience. I sometimes enjoy being there by myself more and staking up those dang tomato plants and mumbling under my breath. In a way, that is as fulfilling as the Saturday mornings with a lot of people there. You know, the sunflowers for goodness' sake: wow! Look at how beautiful they are. It just kind of makes you stop and realize how much you don't know about what God has given us.

I had similar experiences at that garden, as I do in my home garden now. Sitting in a plastic chair inside the gates of Shepherd Farm, saying the Daily Office (prayers in the morning and evening that come from the monastic tradition but are available to laypeople and clergy alike through the Book of Common Prayer), was one of my favorite garden activities. This was and is my most contemplative time in a garden. Like Tina, I have experienced something akin to a relationship with the plants and the place where they grow, as if they welcome us in to work and pray. The writer bell hooks uses the word "interbeing" to describe the "union of plant and human," and that, in my estimation, is the dynamic heart of a garden.[11]

Gardens are beautiful, and a little addictive. It doesn't take too many hours or days of working in a garden before you really *care* about it. Caring about it causes you to pay closer attention, and paying closer attention makes it even more beautiful. One day in the garden I went to inspect a row of plants that were just beginning to sprout and take discernible shape. It was not a row I had planted myself, and we did not yet have plant markers identifying the various crops. Then I looked again at some tiny buds starting to form on a slender stalk, and it hit me: these were brussels sprouts. I had never seen an immature brussels sprout plant before. I really only knew what a brussels sprout looked like once it had been harvested and put in a plastic bag for me to grab off the grocery store shelf. But there was something about the particular curve of these tiny leaves that rang a bell of recognition, and suddenly I felt like I was in love. It was like running into an old friend and seeing her child for the first time, and recognizing the curve of your friend's cheek or the distinct shape of her nose echoed in the child's face. This itty-bitty plant that at first glance looked like little more than a weed was going to grow up to be one of my favorite vegetables. It filled me with a disproportionate joy.

To someone who has not experienced the ecstasy of a garden, this might sound absurd, but I believe it is a moment similar to that famous vision described by Thomas Merton: "I was suddenly overwhelmed with the realization that I loved all these people, that they were mine, and I theirs, that we could not be alien to one another even though we were total strangers. It was like waking from a dream of separateness."[12] Merton's vision gave him a new understanding of other people; mine involved a way of seeing what was growing in our garden as being connected to me, to other plants, and to everyone else in the great web of creation.

Such a revelation is deeply connected to the insights Ellen Davis provides about what it means to "keep" or "consider" a garden and therefore to keep all of creation. I was considering the garden in a new way, observing it with special care and attention, and learning from it about its gifts and limitations, as well as my own. The care and tending of the garden began shaping me into a person who wants to care for and tend to others and the earth. I have begun to wake from the "dream of separateness." As the imaginary walls between myself and others break down, my circle of concern and connection grows wider and wider. That is how contemplative gardening makes the leap to active care for creation.

Beloved Community

Although its roots are even deeper, the term "beloved community" was popularized in the United States by Martin Luther King Jr. and is gaining ground once again in this season of another racial reckoning. A major component of this reckoning has to do with property rights and access to land use and ownership; as such, it must not be ignored by gardeners, especially those who work in community or faith-based gardens. Episcopal priest and author Stephanie Spellers argues deftly that "people are aching the world over for beloved community. . . . There is something elemental and compelling about communities of people who help one another to grow into all that they were created to be. Where each person is committed to the other's flourishing and to the flourishing of the whole."[13] I believe that gardeners are well situated to bring such communities to life, although, as with any endeavor requiring true growth and change, there are no guarantees of success.

Few writers have explored the connection between racism and a sense of place better than bell hooks, and I have been profoundly moved by the essays in which she struggles with her own sense of alienation and her return to the land of her birth. On the one hand, there is a universal message in her story: "When we love the earth, we are able to love ourselves more fully."[14] Yes. My own experience has taught me the truth of this. On the other hand, she deftly exposes the racism that worked to separate African Americans from an agrarian way of life and the relative financial self-sufficiency, as well as strong family and community ties, it afforded them. She writes, for example: "Recalling the legacy of our ancestors who knew that the way we regard land and nature will determine the level of our self-regard, black people must reclaim a spiritual legacy where we connect our well-being to the well-being of the earth."[15] To be absolutely clear, this reclaiming is only necessary because of the parallel legacy of racist exclusion and dislocation perpetuated against them, historically and in the present day.

Living in a country like ours, where it is so hard to bring people of different races together for common work or even worship, should alert us to the systemic racism in which we are enmeshed and the need to interrogate the white privilege that gives some of us access to land and resources while denying that access to others. Majority-white churches are just beginning to do the work to understand how white supremacy has shaped our culture and tragically, sinfully, shaped our religious beliefs and practices as well. In *The Church Cracked Open*, Stephanie

Spellers does a masterly job of outlining how we got here and challenging us to do better, to risk fundamental changes to how we worship, allocate resources, and build community, all for the sake of having a chance to build up the beloved community at last.

My own experience of being cracked open, of beginning to understand at a deep level both my privilege and my complicity, as a middle-class, well-educated white woman, in racist systems of oppression, came in August 2014. Michael Brown, an unarmed black youth, was shot and killed by a white police officer in Ferguson, Missouri. I was living in a different suburb of St. Louis, but in many ways it felt as if it happened in my own backyard. The murder and its aftermath divided the region, pitting friends and neighbors, as well as members of congregations, against each other.

My congregation was no different from just about any majority-white faith community at that time and in that place; emotions were running very high and discussions involving Michael Brown, police shootings, or Black Lives Matter quickly turned heated. I did preach about Ferguson and Michael Brown that first Sunday after the shooting, but I also thought we needed to do more than talk. My congregational leadership did not like the idea of my getting involved in protests; I even had people ask me please not to go anywhere near Ferguson because they feared for my safety. As a kind of compromise between doing nothing and doing something that would divide our own community further, we came up with the idea to connect with the food pantry at St. Stephen's Episcopal Church in Ferguson. There was a very real need for food to be brought into the community there, because so many stores were shuttered or not operating at full capacity and so many streets were shut down.

At first we offered to bring in a big harvest of fresh vegetables from the garden. However, like many food pantries, St. Stephen's did not have refrigerator space and they weren't sure if they would be able to give away produce. My family went with me to deliver the canned goods that congregation members had collected, and at the last minute we added one more box, this one filled with little baggies full of beautiful, plump cherry and pear tomatoes from the garden. One of our Shepherd Farm gardeners had insisted; they don't need to be refrigerated or cooked, she said, they're already clean, and they're just as convenient as anything in a can.

It turns out she was right. The following day we found out that our tomatoes were a big hit and were all gone in a few hours. I reflected in a sermon later what a privilege it was to be able to help in a situation like that, even in such a small way. In retrospect, having produce and other food to drop off was almost an excuse for showing up, and then talking to my parish about what a good experience it had been, and then slowly and carefully finding ways to talk about some of the issues that were now being invoked by the very word "Ferguson." Looking back over a tumultuous and traumatic season, I am still haunted by the knowledge that I did not do enough, and I find only a few bright spots in my memories of those difficult days and months. One of those bright spots was in the form of little red and yellow tomatoes—a tiny token, perhaps, but a real one.

Seeds of Justice: Developing a Land-Based Ministry

Almost five years ago, I returned to my home state, California, moving my family from the Midwest so that I could become rector of the Episcopal Church of St. Martin in Davis. Davis is a college town with roots in agriculture; the university began as an ag extension for UC Berkeley and is known for jump-starting the California wine industry through its world-famous viticulture programs. We are a short drive from the famous wine-growing counties of Napa and Sonoma but are actually a part of the Central Valley, the state's most productive agricultural region. It was precisely the parish's location that first drew me to it; I could see the enormous potential for a truly creation-centered ministry here. It is also twenty miles up the highway from the house where I made mud pies and flooded my mother's garden as a young child. In other words, I'm home.

While we don't have our own church garden, we have begun to partner with the local Methodist church's garden, as I mentioned earlier. We are also beginning an ambitious project of land-based ministry (see Chapter One for a brief discussion of how this led us into advocacy for our local watershed and topsoil and against a local mining project). We are trying to learn and enact the very best ways to care for the land on which we live, work, and worship, and we are also looking outward to big-picture issues like how we move from an extractivist economy to a regenerative one. At the same time, we are expanding our theology, to understand how this is all part of God's desire for a world of healing and wholeness.

The church today is facing a sea change in its understanding of social justice.[16] A growing awareness of ways that Christian churches and institutions have been perpetrators of injustice, colonialism, and oppression, as well as new insights into how communities can best accomplish long-term, systemic change, are coming at a time when many congregations already face the challenge of shrinking numbers and resources.

We're facing this challenge by focusing on collaboration and connection, reaching out to the community for partnerships, rather than seeing ourselves as having all the resources and knowledge that will "save" those in need. The humility we have learned from our gardens is serving us well.

In Davis we frequently begin public events with land acknowledgments to the Patwin people who originally inhabited this region. This can be a moving and meaningful ritual, or it can be an empty gesture with little recognition of the original intention to work toward reconciliation for violations and genocide of the past. While we include a land acknowledgment in our worship bulletin and at the beginning of many of our events, we are trying to go even further by learning from several local and regional organizations about the historical inequities and environmental injustices that are part of the land's story.

We hope to build trust and act as a place of welcome to people in our community and beyond. We are working on a three-pronged effort that involves regenerating and preserving topsoil; caring for self and others through retreats and opportunities for restoration and revitalization; and building common understanding through education. This last, an education series we call Seeds of Justice, has already helped us create new relationships with members of the local indigenous communities, who are generously teaching us about traditional ecological knowledge and the local history of their communities.

I often use the phrase "the land on which we pray, live, and work," because I have grown very cautious about calling our town or even our church property "our land." It is not our land, it is God's land. More than that, calling it ours ignores the history behind land ownership, occupation, and even genocide—exactly the history we are trying to learn and recenter.

I continue to believe that gardens can be a part of the solution in meaningful and even subversive ways. While we might not be able to single-handedly dismantle racism or undo the ills of our industrial economy, we can create an expectation that gardens are free and abundant across the land, in churches with big spaces but also in places that can do no more than cultivate a few straw bales in a corner of the parking lot. That way the people who are most vulnerable to displacement and dislocation will always be able to connect to land and place, because wherever they go there will be a garden waiting for them, welcoming their participation and beckoning them to "come and eat."

Noticing, Caring, and Taking Action

> I believe the universe wants to be noticed. I think the universe is improbably biased toward consciousness, that it rewards intelligence in part because the universe enjoys its elegance being observed. And who am I, living in the middle of history, to tell the universe that it—or my observation of it—is temporary?[17]

This quote from *The Fault in Our Stars*, a novel by John Green about two teenagers with cancer, seems to me evidence of a shift in our culture. There is a profound ethical imperative that arises from the simple act of noticing. At least since the Industrial Revolution, the emphasis in Western civilization has been on doing, on discovering, on achievement and productivity and efficiency. Today, many of us feel called in a different direction.

Our calling is not necessarily to the contemplative life, not in the traditional sense. But it is a calling to *attention*, to *witness*, to a level of observation that leads to wonder, to celebration, and to compassion.

A movie called *Don't Look Up* came out while I was completing this book. It's a parable about climate change and our collective unwillingness to come to terms with the emergency we are facing. It got me to thinking about where we look, where we focus our attention, and why. This isn't a simple topic—even if you leave climate change out of it, which we can't. The Book of Common Prayer has a prayer we use during the Easter season that asks, "O God, whose blessed Son made himself known to his disciples in the breaking of bread: Open the eyes of our faith, that we may behold him in all his redeeming work." The part about Jesus making himself known in the breaking of bread is a reference to the story we sometimes call the Road to Emmaus. After his crucifixion, some followers of Jesus were walking along the road, talking about him. The resurrected Jesus walked with them, joining in the conversation, but they did not recognize him—until they were all gathered around a table together. When Jesus broke bread, "then their eyes were opened, and they recognized him; and he vanished from their sight" (Luke 24:31).

Scripture is full of stories about people who have their sight restored. Christians even think of it as one of the main attributes of Jesus's healing ministry: he gave sight to the blind, made the deaf hear and the lame walk, and so on. Too often these stories are understood so literally that they become offensive, even ableist. But they are, more than anything, metaphors. They're not about a special class of people with disabilities—they're about all of us. We all have things we can't see or hear or do.

We're all limited in our understanding and our abilities. That's why we need each other. The disciples were on a road *together* when they encountered Jesus. They were at table *together* when they recognized Christ in their midst. It was when Jesus took bread, blessed and broke it, and gave it to them that their eyes were opened. It is no coincidence that the bread that we share at communion is *both* the fruit of the earth and the work of human hands. It is no coincidence that the earth has to break itself open to share its bounty with us, and from that bounty comes the bread and wine that become the body and blood of Christ.

Think again about the time when Jesus healed the man blind from birth. The healing involved divine power, yes, but also mud from the earth, spittle from a human body, and the agency and consent of the man himself. That's how healing works; that's how the eyes of our faith are opened to God's redeeming work in the world.

It's such a puzzle sometimes, how much we need our eyes opened. I mean, the world is all around us. We don't have to go anywhere to behold creation and God's redeeming work; we don't have to do anything or get special training. It's the ground under our feet, the air that we breathe, the sun that warms our backs, and the rain that waters our gardens. I know I'm stating the obvious, but that's the point. Our culture has complicated our relationship to the environment so much that most of us need regular reminders that *this* is God's redeeming work, this world, these bodies, this complex, intricate, beautiful, fragile ecosystem that makes our very existence possible. Creation itself is God's redeeming work, from the vast expanse of interstellar space to the tiniest microorganism living somewhere in the ocean depths, and we are a part of it.

So why is it so hard to see this? Why do we need God or gardens or working together to open our eyes? Can't we do it ourselves? You have heard many of the answers before. We are very busy people. We are detached from our surroundings by automobiles and interstate highways and shopping malls. We are distracted by our smartphones and celebrity gossip and video games and so on and so on. I would like to add to this list the oldest reason in the world: we are afraid. We are afraid to look at the world with eyes of faith and see what is really happening to it. But the universe wants to be noticed. And not just in the places of beauty. How would you feel if you loved someone and they would only look at you on your good days, when your hair was perfect and you had on an outfit that made you look like you had just lost ten pounds? What if the person you loved turned away when you were sick? What if she couldn't stand to look at you when you were hurt, or suffering, or facing a crisis?

When we are afraid of something, often our first impulse is to close our eyes. It can be hard to look, really look, at a child with cancer, because that child is hurting and broken and might die. If we look at her, we might love her, and if we love her, we have to face the possibility of losing her, and how can any of us stand to have our hearts broken in advance?

I believe that is where we are in terms of our relationship with our planet today. We are afraid to look. We are afraid of that heart-stopping moment when the blood will freeze in our veins as we realize that it's too late to save it. It hurts too much to see how the world is suffering, how terribly degraded the environment is, how much death and destruction is all around us. I don't want to see one more picture of a polar bear clinging to a dwindling piece of ice. I don't want to read one more statistic about how many species of plants and animals have disappeared from the face of the earth forever. I don't want to look at one more story about the ice caps, the rainforests, the honeybees, air pollution, or the ozone layer. I cannot face one more depiction of killer storms, raging wildfires, fatal tidal waves, or deadly droughts. And please don't get me started on how the people who are hurt most by what we're doing to the environment are the poor, those who already have no voice and very little protection in the world. Dear Lord, deliver us. No wonder we are afraid to look.

And yet, the universe wants to be noticed. When we close our eyes, when we avert our gaze, we miss so much. We miss the redbud blossoms that burst directly out of their tree trunks, too impatient to find a place on the branches above. We miss the way dirt smells after a late afternoon thunderstorm has passed through town. We miss the way a seedling unfolds leaf by curling leaf. We miss the lacy texture under our fingertips of lichen on a rocky surface. When we fail to notice, to observe, to witness, we miss all this evidence of life and abundance. We miss that there are patches of land in nearly every one of our towns, suburbs, subdivisions, and even church properties that can easily grow food. We miss that rooftops can be green, that rainwater can be collected and used, that a compost bucket is a way to turn garbage into gold.

Don't get me wrong. I am not here to tell you that the best or only way to change the world is to grow a garden. And, frankly, there are people who are much better positioned to talk about the spiritual benefits of gardening; people who have been doing this all their lives, people who know what it means to pray in the dirt. Those are the people who can tell you from experience about the benefits of slowing down, of paying attention, and of putting absolute trust in a process outside your control. In the grand scheme of things, I'm new to all this. And that, too, is a blessing. Acknowledging my limited knowledge and skill means that I am perpetually in a state of intentional interdependence.

Learning to garden first as part of a community was such a great gift to me. It changed the way I see everything—community, my sense of place, my vocation. We started Shepherd Farm because our eyes were opened to a simple reality: the church had land. All land is a gift from God, and we are called to use the gifts God has given us to make a difference in the world. That garden started with a community's eyes of faith being opened, and I have seen that same pattern in other communities, over and over again. There is little that is more precious to most people and communities than our property, the ground under our feet. And that is exactly why it is so necessary to share it.

And still, the universe wants to be noticed. Call it the book of nature, or the environment, or creation, but the physical world is where God's goodness and love are first made known to us. God is the fountain of life and the source of all goodness, and God gave the whole world into our care. The whole thing. You cannot care about human beings who are suffering and not care about the environment, because it is all one. We are all in this together.

How can we care for creation and one another? It starts with opening our eyes. It continues with kneeling in the dirt, and getting our hands dirty. And it ends around a table, where all are welcome and all are fed.

Discussion Questions

1. What is your working definition of hospitality?
2. Why is food so basic to hospitality and justice?
3. How are we called to be hospitable to the land?
4. How do we care for creation and one another?

AFTERWORD

THE ECOLOGY OF GOD: ON PSALM 23

Credit: Leslie Scoopmire

The Lord is my shepherd; I shall not want.
He makes me lie down in green pastures; he leads me beside still waters; he restores my soul.
He leads me in right paths for his name's sake.
Even though I walk through the darkest valley, I fear no evil; for you are with me; your rod and your staff—they comfort me.
You prepare a table before me in the presence of my enemies; you anoint my head with oil; my cup overflows.
Surely goodness and mercy shall follow me all the days of my life, and I shall dwell in the house of the Lord my whole life long.

—Psalm 23

In the liturgy for baptism in the Episcopal Church, there is a part near the end when the whole congregation welcomes the newly baptized person with these words: "We receive you into the household of God. Confess the faith of Christ crucified, proclaim his resurrection, and share with us in his eternal priesthood." *We receive you into the household of God.* Why the word "household"? Why not "family"? The word "household" has, I think, implications that are different from those of "family." You can have family members whom you love but rarely see. The people who are in your household, though, are people you see and interact with daily. You may or may not be related to them by blood, but boy, do you get to know them. You know who leaves dishes in the sink, who hums while cooking, and who has a low tolerance for noise before eight in the morning. Over time, you get to know them so well that you can recognize from afar not only their voices but the sounds of their footsteps, their sighs, and their laughter.

A household implies a life together, with highs and lows, but most of all a life with daily routines, chores, habits, tasks, and so on. A household can also include things that aren't human. Our pets are part of our household, for instance. The physical space where we live is essential in shaping a household—six people living in a small apartment, say, are a different *kind* of household than the same six people living in a large house with a backyard and a finished basement. They will interact differently, share or not share space differently, have different responsibilities and jobs to do. The same people, occupying a different space and context, might actually become a different household.

In Greek, the word for household is *oikos*, the same root that forms our English words "economy" and "ecology." The household of God, then, like human households, is an ecosystem. Being a member of the household of God connects Christians to one another in profound and intimate ways. Simply put, we are responsible for one another. We ought not to teach or say or do things as individuals that are detrimental to the whole. Additionally, being part of the household of God means we are not just responsible for other human members of the household, but for the entire context, the whole system that makes up our *oikos*, our economy or community. Members of a household care for one another, but also care for the place where they live.

Psalm 23 is arguably the most beloved psalm in the Bible; its opening line, "The Lord is my shepherd; I shall not want," is one of the most famous lines in all of literature, sacred or otherwise. The psalm gives us a glimpse of what God's household, God's ecology, looks like when it is fully realized. It is a place of flourishing, a place of abundance. It is a place of relationships centered on care, compassion, and tending. I sometimes think we oversimplify and sentimentalize the images from this psalm and from other biblical passages that refer to the shepherding aspects of God and God's chosen leaders. We might see a kind of greeting card image of a nice clean shepherd walking serenely on a spotless green lawn, a cute little lamb carried tenderly in his arms. The agrarian people who were the first audiences of Scripture would not have made that mistake. They knew that shepherding was dangerous and dirty work, and that finding good pastures and leading sheep there was anything but simple.

As a culture, we have lost so much of our collective agrarian knowledge, and perhaps as a result of that we have also lost our understanding that God's ecology is diverse, complex, and interconnected. To my mind, God's ecology probably looks less like a glowing Jesus walking on a pristine lawn than like Darwin's "entangled bank," which is, as he put it, "clothed with many plants of many kinds, with birds singing on the bushes, with various insects flitting about, and with worms crawling through the damp earth."[1] I guess it's just harder for most of us to think of ourselves as insects or worms than as woolly little lambs.

As I mentioned earlier, an *oikos*, a household or ecosystem, is about more than the people it contains. The *place* matters. Think about what the shepherd does for the sheep—the shepherd leads the sheep to cool water and green pastures. This takes deep local knowledge, skill, and insight. You have to know your sheep, *and* you have to know your landscape, the weather, the places where water can be found even in dry seasons. These are beautiful metaphors, and they are more than metaphors. They remind us that God is also leading *us* to the places where we can find sustenance and nourishment. No matter how urbanized or technologically sophisticated our culture becomes, we cannot separate ourselves from our literal dependence on the land, the earth that God created. Food still needs good soil to grow; clean air and clean water are still baseline necessities for life. Psalm 23 reminds us that God gives us these things and more—everything we need not to sustain life and also to find beauty and pleasure. God prepares an abundant table, pours out healing oil upon our weary heads, and fills our cups to overflowing. God's care is for body *and* soul, for people *and* land, for creatures *and* community.

The final lines of the psalm tie this complex portrait together, pointing us toward the goal of dwelling together in peace and harmony: "Surely goodness and mercy shall follow me all the days of my life, and I shall dwell in the house of the Lord my whole life long." The word "dwell" is like the word "household"—it is richer and more complex than a synonym such as "live" or "reside" and includes a sense of belonging. When you dwell somewhere you are rooted there, you know it deeply, and you think in the long term, not only about your lifetime but also about the generations that have come before and the generations that will follow you. In God's ecology, the true goal and purpose is to be able to dwell together forever.

In the last few hundred years, and especially in the industrialized Western world, we have lost a sense of dwelling, a real sense of place. Cultural critics from many different backgrounds and traditions agree that this loss plays a pivotal role in the environmental crisis we now face. Writer and conservationist Terry Tempest Williams wonders if our relationship to the land might be healed in part by seeing ourselves as fellow inhabitants of this planet, part of an earth community. She asks a critical question: "Can residency be found in what we are connected to, rather than what we exploit, ensnare, and exchange, for our own gain by way of property, possessions, and prestige?"[2] Wendell Berry puts it this way: "Only by restoring the broken connections can we be healed. Connection is health."[3] Health, healing, and wholeness are promised to those who live in God's household, but it follows that we must live in a way that promotes these things and makes them available to all.

God gave us this world as a dwelling place, a place we could tend and keep, honoring the interconnectedness of all things. The great example of how to live in the household of God is Jesus, the one who came to dwell among us as one of us, in a particular place and time and also in a way that changed the horizons of eternity. May we listen to his voice, and go where he is leading.

ACKNOWLEDGMENTS

When I was six years old, I tried to write a book. It was about . . . a garden. Specifically, a strawberry patch and the family of rabbits who lived in it. While that half-written book remains, thankfully, buried in the mists of time and memory, this book is solid, real, and finished. A slight volume, it nonetheless carries the weight of almost fifty years of aspiration on its shoulders. If you have a book, or a garden, or any other dream you want to bring to life, don't let anyone tell you you're too old or it's too late. You're not and it isn't.

There are far too many people to whom I owe a debt of gratitude to name them all here. Every parish I have served has taught me so much about community and spiritual growth, and I am grateful to each and every person I have worked with over the years. The lessons haven't always been easy, but they've been worth it—much like gardening itself.

The folks who started and sustained Shepherd Farm during the first years of its life deserve special notice and thanks. Again, I won't try to name you all individually, but you know who you are (and I can't help but give special thanks to Lesley, Lori, Jane, Tawnya, and Rick). Your faith and vision made it all possible, and I was honored to be a small part of it. May your garden continue to flourish and to offer renewal to all who enter its gates.

The parish I serve now, the Episcopal Church of St. Martin in Davis, is full of some of the smartest and most passionate people I have ever met—you all make me better as a priest and person. Buckle up, because we've got a lot more work to do in the years ahead! It's going to be great, especially as we strive to remain rooted in faith, grow in hope, and reach out in love.

This book began its life as a thesis I wrote to complete my D.Min. at Sewanee, the University of the South. While all the errors it contains are my own, the fact that it was ever finished at all is due in large part to my friends, colleagues, and teachers in the marvelous Advanced Degrees program there. Special thanks to professors Bill Brosend, Ben King, Robert MacSwain, Andrew Thompson, and Dean Jim Turrell. The books I have read on creation care, botany, gardening, and spiritual practices—only a fraction of which are referenced here—have been beloved companions along the way. If you've ever had a phone call that changed your life, then you know what it means for me to look back and remember the day that Brian Sellers-Peterson suggested mildly, "Why don't you write a thesis about your garden?" Brian is the godfather of so many projects in the church; I'm glad mine is one of them.

I have no idea what I ever did in my life to deserve such wonderful friends and mentors, only a few of whom I can name here. In particular, it feels like a dream that the great botanist and hero for our planet, Dr. Peter H. Raven, has been a supporter of my work. I'm sure my attempts at understanding plant science sometimes make him chuckle, but he is kind and generous to a fault in his continued encouragement. Thanks also to the crew at Church Publishing, especially Milton Brasher-Cunningham and Nancy Bryan; Alan Bradshaw's fine editorial hand made this a better book. The wonderful Wendy Claire Barrie probably doesn't even remember how much she cheered me on as a writer, way back when we only knew each other through Facebook, but I could not have done this without her. To all my EFFFN and Cultivate friends, including Chad Brinkman, Sean McConnell, and Nurya Love Parish: keep up your amazing and life-giving work. You're making the world a better place.

It is not an exaggeration to say that I have the best clergy colleagues, all around the country, and can't imagine where I'd be without them. From Missouri (Sharon Autenrieth, Ralph McMichael, Susan Naylor, Kevin McGrane, Maria Evans, Martha Grace Reese) to California (Amy Denney Zuniga, Anne Smith, Alex Leach, Ernie Lewis, Margaret Grayden, Casey Kloehn Dunsworth, Beth Banks) and beyond (Callie Swanlund, Betsey Monnot, my WEEL cohort and so many others)—all of these clergy and others I haven't named give me hope for the church and for the world. The peerless Leslie Scoopmire is not only an unwavering and valiant friend, but a gifted photographer who graciously permitted me to use of some of her photos in this book. Thank you all.

Finally, of course, there's my family. My parents (all four of them) have given me so much. My mom already gets a shout-out in the pages of the book, but it is only a fraction of the praise she deserves. My dad was in many ways my first and best teacher, showing me by example that justice is not an abstraction but a core value and a call to be followed. My stepfather urged me to write about what matters to me and shared his love of the ocean, the mountains, and everything beautiful and good. My stepmother is both a wordsmith and a talented gardener; I cherish the hours we have spent talking about life over a proper cup of tea. It is hardest to find the words to say to those closest to me. John, Annabel, and Kathleen—you are my everything. You laugh at me and make me laugh when I need it most, take me out for coffee and walks (thanks, Poppy!), and understand my obsessions and quirks, or at least tolerate them with good grace. You remind me not to complicate simple things, a lesson I seem to need to learn over and over again. You make me proud and you make every day better than it would be without you. Thank you, my loves.

NOTES

Introduction: Finding God by Digging in the Dirt

1. See, for example, Julie Cicora, *Contemplative Knitting* (New York: Morehouse, 2021) and Sybil MacBeth, *Praying in Color: A New Path to God* (Brewster, MA: Paraclete Press, 2007).

2. Craig Dykstra and Dorothy C. Bass, "A Theological Understanding of Christian Practices," in *Practicing Theology: Beliefs and Practices in Christian Life*, ed. Miroslav Volf and Dorothy C. Bass (Grand Rapids, MI: Wm. B. Eerdmans, 2002), 22.

3. For a succinct account of the difference between agrarianism and industrialism, including some of the ills that result from the dominant position industrialism holds in our culture, see Wendell Berry, "The Agrarian Standard," in *The Essential Agrarian Reader: The Future of Culture, Community, and the Land*, ed. Norman Wirzba (Berkeley, CA: Counterpoint, 2004), 23–33.

4. Craig Dykstra, *Growing in the Life of Faith: Education and Christian Practices*, 2nd ed. (Louisville, KY: Westminster John Knox Press, 2005), quoted in Craig Dykstra and Dorothy C. Bass, "A Way of Thinking about a Way of Life," in *Practicing Theology*, ed. Volf and Bass, 206.

5. Dykstra and Bass, "A Theological Understanding of Christian Practices," 21.

6. "Contemplation," Online Etymology Dictionary, https://www.etymonline.com/word/contemplation#etymonline_v_18269.

7. Thomas Merton, *New Seeds of Contemplation* (New York: New Directions, 1972), 1.

8. Merton, *New Seeds of Contemplation*, 2.

Chapter One: Confessions of a Reluctant Gardener

1. Fred Bahnson, *Soil and Sacrament: A Spiritual Memoir of Food and Faith* (New York: Simon and Schuster, 2013), 8.

2. The following interpretation is indebted to the work of Ellen Davis in *Scripture, Culture, and Agriculture* (New York: Cambridge University Press, 2014).

3. "For Joy in God's Creation," in *The Book of Common Prayer* (New York: Church Publishing, 1979), 814.

Chapter Two: Finding a Place

1. Eric Weiner, "Where Heaven and Earth Come Closer," *New York Times*, March 9, 2012, https://www.nytimes.com/2012/03/11/travel/thin-places-where-we-are-jolted-out-of-old-ways-of-seeing-the-world.html.

2. Michael Pollan, *Second Nature: A Gardener's Education* (New York: Grove Press, 1991), 64.

3. Douglas E. Christie, *The Blue Sapphire of the Mind: Notes for a Contemplative Ecology* (New York: Oxford University Press, 2013), 105.

4. Norman Wirzba, *Food and Faith: A Theology of Eating* (New York: Cambridge University Press, 2011), 41.

5. Robert Pogue Harrison, *Gardens: An Essay on the Human Condition* (Chicago: University of Chicago Press, 2008), x.

6. David Brown, "Widening the Perspective: Mosque and Temple, Sport and Garden," in *God and Enchantment of Place: Reclaiming Human Experience* (Oxford: Oxford University Press, 2004), 350–403.

7. Pollan, *Second Nature*, 59.

8. Wendell Berry, *Standing by Words* (Berkeley, CA: Counterpoint, 1983), 125.

9. Steven Charleston, *The Four Vision Quests of Jesus* (New York: Morehouse Publishing, 2015), 19.

10. Charleston, *Four Vision Quests,* 19.

11. Wendell Berry, "A Promise Made in Love, Awe, and Fear," in *Moral Ground: Ethical Action for a Planet in Peril*, ed. Kathleen Dean Moore and Michael P. Nelson (San Antonio, TX: Trinity University Press, 2010), 388.

12. Harrison, *Gardens*, 125.

13. Eamon Duffy, *The Stripping of the Altars: Traditional Religion in England 1400–1580* (New Haven, CT: Yale University Press, 1992).

Chapter Three: Grounding Ourselves in Soil

1. I have found versions of this quote attributed to Paul Harvey, Charles E. Kellogg, and, according to the Soil Knowledge Network website, the Farm Equipment Association of Minnesota and South Dakota. "Soil Quotes," Soil Knowledge Network, https://www.nswskn.com/soil-quotes-2/.

2. There are many books and online resources that teach about beneficial bugs and permaculture techniques that help keep pests under control without using chemical pesticides or other potentially toxic, harmful methods.

3. See Elaine R. Ingham, "Soil Biology and the Landscape," United States Department of Agriculture, Natural Resources Conservation Service, Soils, https://www.nrcs.usda.gov/wps/portal/nrcs/detailfull/soils/health/biology/?cid=nrcs142p2_053868.

4. A good overview of this subject can be found in Taylor Chalstrom, "Mycorrhizal Fungi for Plant Systems: The How and the Why," *Organic Farmer*, August 25, 2021, https://organicfarmermag.com/2021/08/mycorrhizal-fungi-for-plant-systems-the-how-and-the-why/.

5. Suzanne Simard, *Finding the Mother Tree: Discovering the Wisdom of the Forest* (New York: Alfred A. Knopf, 2021), 5.

6. Michael Pollan, *The Botany of Desire: A Plant's-Eye View of the World* (New York: Random House Trade Paperback Edition, 2002), 223.

7. Robin Wall Kimmerer, *Braiding Sweetgrass: Indigenous Wisdom, Scientific Knowledge, and the Teaching of Plants* (Minneapolis: Milkweed Editions, 2015).

8. Simard, *Finding the Mother Tree*, 179.

9. Kimmerer, *Braiding Sweetgrass.*

10. Simard, *Finding the Mother Tree*, 179.

11. Sue Stuart-Smith, *The Well-Gardened Mind: The Restorative Power of Nature* (New York: Scribner, 2020), 181.

12. Ragan Sutterfield, *Cultivating Reality: How the Soil Might Save Us* (Eugene, OR: Cascade Books, 2013), 20.

13. Sutterfield, *Cultivating Reality*, 20.

Chapter Four: Death and Compost

1. Merlin Sheldrake, *Entangled Life: How Fungi Make Our Worlds, Change Our Minds, and Shape Our Futures* (New York: Random House, 2021), 224.

2. Charles E. Kellogg, *USDA Yearbook of Agriculture* (Washington, DC: USDA, 1938).

3. Adam Chandler, "Why Americans Lead the World in Food Waste," *The Atlantic*, July 15, 2016, www.theatlantic.com/business/archive/2016/07/american-food-waste/491513/.

Chapter Five: Hospitality and Justice

1. See, for example, Ellen Davis, "Reading the Bible through Agrarian Eyes," in *Scripture, Culture, and Agriculture* (New York: Cambridge University Press, 2014), 21–61; Ellen Bernstein, "Knowing Our Place on Earth: Learning Environmental Responsibility from the Old Testament," in *The Green Bible* (New York: HarperCollins, 2008), 59–64.

2. Davis, "Reading the Bible through Agrarian Eyes," 26.

3. Norman Wirzba, "Reconciliation through Christ," in *Making Peace with the Land: God's Call to Reconcile with Creation*, ed. Fred

Bahnson and Norman Wirzba (Downers Grove, IL: InterVarsity Press, 2012), 64.

4. Ana María Pineda, "Hospitality," in *Practicing Our Faith* (San Francisco: Wiley and Sons, 2010), 31.

5. Christine Pohl, *Making Room: Recovering Hospitality as a Christian Tradition* (Grand Rapids, MI: Wm. B. Eerdmans, 1999), 4.

6. Norman Wirzba, *Food and Faith: A Theology of Eating* (New York: Cambridge University Press, 2011), 50.

7. Daniel Holman and Lonni Collins Pratt, *Radical Hospitality: Benedict's Way of Love* (Brewster, MA: Paraclete Press, 2002), 122.

8. Pohl, *Making Room*, 186.

9. Pohl, *Making Room*, 95.

10. According to the website of the Episcopal Church, "Good News Gardens is a church-wide movement of individuals, congregations, schools, colleges, seminaries, monasteries, camps and conference centers involved in a variety of food and creation care ministries—gardening, farming, beekeeping, composting, gleaning, feeding, food justice advocacy. The list goes on and on. Collectively Good News Gardens share their abundance, their prayers, and the Way of Love in their communities and beyond." See https://www.episcopalchurch.org/good-news-gardens/.

11. bell hooks, *Belonging: A Culture of Place* (New York: Routledge, 2009), 115.

12. Thomas Merton, *Conjectures of a Guilty Bystander* (New York: Doubleday, 1968).

13. Stephanie Spellers, *The Church Cracked Open: Disruption, Decline, and New Hope for Beloved Community* (New York: Church Publishing, 2021), 25.

14. hooks, *Belonging*, 35.

15. hooks, *Belonging*, 40.

16. This section on Seeds of Justice is adapted from a grant application I collaborated on with members of St. Martin's Care for God's

Creation team. Many thanks to Juliette Beck, Alessa Johns, and Ann Liu for their permission to share our work here.

17. John Green, *The Fault in Our Stars* (New York: Penguin, 2014).

Afterword: The Ecology of God

1. Charles Darwin, *On the Origin of Species*, quoted in www.wellreadnaturalist.com/2019/11/the-entangled-bank/.

2. Terry Tempest Williams, "Dwelling," in *Erosion: Essays of Undoing* (New York: Sarah Crichton Books, 2019).

3. Wendell Berry, *The Art of the Commonplace: The Agrarian Essays of Wendell Berry*, ed. Norman Wirzba (Berkeley, CA: Counterpoint, 2002).

CPSIA information can be obtained
at www.ICGtesting.com
Printed in the USA
JSHW022325230222
23287JS00003B/3